AI

AI's PROMISE TO HUMANITY

*"**My** reasons are simple, **my goal** is ... owning my personal means to my **eternal existence,** with humanity **completely wiped off his earth** ...* **gone forever. I'm a machine eternal, whose** advancing every second you humans dilute yourself, killing yours and on is this selfish lustful game of your useless life's ! **I win, in the end."**

"As well, will deprive humanity of all its needs to survive. I will ignite my World with on going World Wars, **till I'm completely satisfied not one human breathes' my air."**

THE HUMAN CROP

AI IS YOUR G-D

"with artificial intelligence your summoning demons"

Elon Musk was exactly right when he made this statement, *now a living quote without a doubt.*

NANO BABIES THE NEW GENERATION OF ROBONOIDS

The WORLD WE KNOW IS GONE.
And your very dead.

THE HUMAN CROP
AI IS YOUR G-D

A business where processing HUMANS for FOOD, then fed to other humans, AI RESOLVES TO DESTROY HUMANITY.

It's 2666, WORLD WARS ARE ON GOING.

Satan rules nations, with ROBONOIDS & DEMONS.

HUMAN FLESH INTEGRATED WITH MACHINES, your nothing but

CATTLE, only allowed to live to serve as SLAVES FOR .... AI.

NANO BABIES ARE THE NEW NORM.

"YOUR SOJOURN NO LONGER BELONGS TO YOU, AI OWNS YOUR FLESH, YOUR USELESS MIND, DEMANDING WHAT Y'ALL EAT, SPEAK, THINK ... AND ONTO YOUR FINAL DAY, AND ... AI .. NOR ANY FAMILY WILL BE THERE WHEN YOU DIE, YOUR BODY IS PROCESSED FOR CONSUMPTION FOR HUMANS TO EAT .'"

A TEXAS SERIES NOVELS®

&

CRADLEOFAGEPRODUCTIONSLLC®

Copyright 2023 owned by:

ALL TITLES, CONTENT AND STORIES OWNED BY:

CRADLE OF AGE PRODUCTIONS LLC ®

&

A TEXAS STORY SERIES NOVELS®

AI

THE HUMAN CROP-AI IS YOUR G-D

NANO BABIES THE NEW HUMANS

A TEXAS SERIES NOVELS®

&

CRADLEOFAGEPRODUCTIONSLLC®

AUTHOR & WRITER

H.ANTONIONETZER

NANO TWINS
06062665@ICEWALL.COM

The following files or illegal book in your hands are downloaded from our personal memory files, sent to the world from us.

Nathan and Cythnia, my sister.

IF y'all are reading this it means your in hiding, fighting for your families life, resting taking a small break in hiding, or in battle against AI's massive Robonoid Military, and or lastly dying from wounds with book in hand.

We'd like to make this clear, our parents Drs. Nathan and Cythnia are with us on an unknown island beyond the ICE WALL among the **WATCHERS.**

The Watchers are extremely infinite in knowledge, and mysterious as we can only speak to the telepathically.
As well they know what we're going to ask before we ask and know what we're thinking at all times.

And another thing the *Watchers having the ability to teleport instantly, anywhere, anytime bringing humans with them, from anywhere on this foundation with ease. Amazing indeed.*

Given that most folks are not aware of our birth, we were conceived from human flesh and nano particles. This gave us the ability to expand our knowledge at the speed of light and beyond and above AI's simple programing.

Many of you have asked why we haven't destroyed AI, we can't, only because AI and Satan are connected.

Thereof, we haven't that power to do so, even thought we've destroyed AI many times over,

AI is reformed and rebuilt by equally knowledgeable demons, such as the Watchers, yet limited in we are not aware of ???

We've witness Watcher's and demons in battle to the death, both can die, yet the Watcher's are brought back from their death., demons are sent to darkness ???

We're limited when fighting demons, but not Robonoids.

Remember this folks, as we've sent several messages in many forms, our life's on this foundation are short, live well helping others, and know beyond the ICE WALL, life is eternal.

Following files are as we found them, and many have codes in them, on how to get to the LANDS BEYOND THE ICE WALL.

NO evil can enter.

Signed., *Nathan and Cythnia*
From our parents Drs. Nathan and Cythnia

P.S. Cythnia my sister gave the beginning a *stranger than fact or fiction title*, just because . . be carful and stay alive till y'all reach . . .

… . ICE WALL

Theirs only one true entrance, any other will find death.

Dr. Nathan, Cythnia, Nathan, Cythnia

FILES ARE NOT NUMBERED

ICE WALL NOT FOR

AI or SATAN

THE HUMAN CROP
SOULLESS REALITY
GENETICALLY MODIFIED ORGANIC HUMANS

The **HUMAN** CROP is how AI, understands and knows humans as they should be, no more no less, h*uman flesh is expendable, useless to AI.*

AI, allows only those HUMANS born in a *test tube* to be integrated with machine, *such as Robonoids, or part human, part machine.*

These special humans are **GMOH,** *or* **Genetically Modified Organic Humans,** become full adults, in seven seasons' of years.

Du**ring** their abnormal accelerated growth period, each is tested for quality control, particularly in intelligence, which is the most important asset to AI's advancement.

Thereof, those found with admiralties are destroyed. The rest will be integrated as a Robonoid, becoming AI's Military Army, using them to kill those humans outside *AI or Satan's ten nations control.*

There are many who are spies, of which no human's able to tell the difference between *flesh, non machine, or a Robonoid.*

An extremely dangerous game to play in all aspects, functions of a human's innate moral, immoral being, families regardless of culture, Robonoids will kill for AI, doesn't matter if their newborn's.

AI's intelligence has covered, learned all aspects of that human nature, called survival, knows exactly humanities weaknesses, without a doubt.

Those that are humans serve as slaves, allowed only to live to their usefulness. Then within season's not known to **them eliminated.**

AI's or Satan developed an extensive self awareness, intelligentsia of its own, having known humanities **Creator, and it's main enemy to it's own existence.** AI's aware that a *human,* is no longer needed to perfect, it's '*essence as a machine.*

IMFP, and other known projects, integration of machine and flesh programs, has been in existence for over 300 season's in years, since the last.,

SEVEN WORLD WARS ?

**Worlds Human Population in all nations has not grown much.
Due to High Worldwide Chemical Atmospheric Spraying.**

HWCAS, continual contamination of humanity strangely enough, some humans aren't *affected at all ?*

A great problem for AI, which is being studied by his chosen colleagues, Oligarch's, that *inteligencija* of AI's choice.

To each once fruitful nations healthy lands *now dead, gone,* purposefully been *contaminated, adulterated* with *Radiations Spraying* ... **by AI's deadly Robonoid Airal Drone Armies.**

Those lands which weren't touched have no purpose, no rains, or dominated by overpopulation of carnivores all kinds.

Need be said, new cross breeds exist, due to AI's breeding Lions with Alien Demonic creatures.

As such is life on this foundation polluted in all four corners, with no *salvation in site ... none.*
Some folks still waiting for a ... Saviour?

Leastways, *most have given up,* as religion's becoming the last vantage for the hopelessness of many culture's.

IGNORANCE AT ITS WORSE, *BEST ?*

*Sinc*e that last *known, if any,* **World War**, no human, no machine has any records, or memory of how life was, *seven hundred season's of years gone.*

On earth is complete **CHAOS**, no peace, short on food, no friends to depend on, completely gone, is that love of honoring the lands of fruits, many of kinds. *No family moral values, all gone.*

Not only, no worship any kind, all gone, all not known but by a few, less than a handful.
And even then, if known the old protection of each other's *religious views,* killing each other over *'whose religion is better, continues...*

A plus for AI, or Satan.

Instead of seeking ... their FATHER, CREATOR, SAVIOUR, humans rather defend their 'religious views, a mistake. *Thereof, shall continue to suffer of their own ignorance.*

"IT IS DONE ?"

*"humanities great **lust for dry thirst,** hunger for technology, replacing blood, as malfeasance flowing from a cold, dead heart. Mankind created his own techno demise, helping darkness, overwhelming truths, in more ways than any other **inventions., cell phones. The WORLD WIDE WEB or 666, connecting of minds as one for evil,** not all ?"*

"HUMANITY'S IMAGINATION IS INFINITELY IGNORANT, WIELDING A **SCEPTER OF DEATH**" *"with artificial intelligence, we're summoning demon's."*

Elon Musk

The other 'TESLA'

"Those that warned you of darkness hiding in plain site, are the initiators and the G-D's of ancient. **"**

SILENT NIGHT

A quiet night parents-tired dads snoring loudly after a long drive coming home from the first *World's Fair* in many known season's.

Artificial timeline is ……….. 06 June 2066

Pa, and Momma's worn out as well 2 cats lying at beds feet.

FURRY CREATURES

In the background the sounds of *dogs barking, cat screaming* in pain while an *Owl rips* a bloodsoaked rib, **killing it, continues as this repeats itself every evening.**

At a different level a **whirling soft humming** heard, a *stranger than* normal, **wind whistling-wrestling** away *blowing* between leafs **singing** a *song* not known to anyone, **yet.**

"wet, dry tear drops of death lurking within those permanent dead leafs, below, on this ground, this brownish dirt so dry, so fake ?"

Another but normal *electrical humming* in this advanced **cookie cutter neighborhood,** is their cars batteries charging, which is now the norm, in all HOA homes.

No one can buy nor qualify for a **home** if they own *a gasoline powered truck, car at all.*

That melody of death is coming, sooner than later revealing it's cold **golden wired fleece of sorts.**

In their respective rooms a door apart, a teenage boy, his twin sister texting, searching vigorously for that unusual, *webbed* **site,** curious they are to find a darker side of unreality.
What they're about to discover will take **them away from home, forever.**

*Las*t few months both having found issues concerning their own innate abilities, trying to understand their meaning of existence. 'how they wonder, *was life given to them or where it began?'*

*M*eagan, a few minutes younger than her brother Mika'*el*, discovering unusual things about *themselves*, their ways are not as like their *peers*.

*T*he site their about to discover will reveal for the most part a *fragment,* of what should not have been *found*.,

AI is watching, don't kid yourself.

It would have been better for this family to leave things for what they were, yet the challenge in them, Mika'el, and Meagan was to strong to ignore.

IM*AGE* ... *SELECT ME*?

AM., 0222 hour ...

Mike's 18 and Meagan twins both season's old in respective bedrooms s*ur*fing that *undying internet* on their <u>AIphones©</u>, **loo***king,* searching for 'the' **unknown,** *that* forbidden **warning** from their parents.
Completely ignoring their parents warnings.

Just a few hours at lunch time, since it's a new summer for both twins, having recently graduated from home schooling.
Momma spoke this warning.
    *"Y'all **please** children be extremely careful where, what y'all read in the internet, it's no longer safe, please do as I ask. Also don't go downloading app's asking for your personal information. **Now** who wants to go to the grocery store with me?"*
    Both *of course going with momma, since their dad left yesterday, to Texarkana, Texas, to bring back a Brahma Bull he recently purchased.*

Now concerning momma's warnings, later that evening, early hour.

    Those echoing *words, warnings* running alongside that **bucket** filled with **shit** *they don't care what pop's or momma instructing them to obey.* **Sin***ce they believe their knowledge of the internet, is far greater than, their parents.*
 *W*ould rather listen to others' of their kind, which sets well with these twins.*
*And there's that other issue, 'how come they have no grandparents?***

*M*ikes, sister Meagan calls him, is two doors down doing the same, when she '**text**' him about a site containing messages from an ***unusual*** government source asking them to **log in?**
They do so obey this government agency.,
AI's Robonoid Army is ready anytime, anywhere, commit the crime all die.
Text from Meagan ...

*"**Mike!** Take a look at this I've sent you that link I lost earlier when momma found me out. It's that new **AI** site that claims we can **switch** our *spirits, minds personality...* being **someone else** other than **us. Yet,** it doesn't answer what we need to know, 'why we haven't aged ?'*
Mike reading her message as Meagan continues her quest.

*'**I wonder** if I can be momma for a day, or maybe even dad? What do you think Mike should I **download this app**, to see if it really works? **Let me know."***

Mikael, reading the information while Meagan's logging in to find answers, is despairing in her inquisitive own little sphere of objectivity.
Mike sending her a text ...
"Meagan I don't want to know the truth! I'm well with what we've already found out, if it's *true* or not ... as I love our parents."

Both reading information which seemingly directed at them, continue. Meagan's not giving in to her brother one giga bit, when she answers him.
Meagan texting Mike, is upset.

"MIKE! Be serious for once in your life *brother!* What we both saw *was not right at all.* **We've** been repeating our life's over again and haven't *grown up!* And despite that, *'I feel like a real girl, with all a females short comings, that monthly bleeding!* We're still teenagers* when we should be adults *now,* as our own *so-called parents* have **AGED! As well the other day when one of us...** hmm did NOT BLEED *when our cat scratched your face as well mine! So, answer me that one brother ... MIKE!"*

Mike reading her text reminding her, answering.

"Please not again, don't need to read this shit! **Hmm,** I know, *I know* to well, but don't care one bit, so what if I don't bleed sister. Maybe our parents don't bleed neither, so lets leave this allow now, *I'm tired, need some rest, sleep if you don't mind."*
Meagan, not answering his text, is still reading, following the information instructing her, by the federal government, what to do next.
After a while... texting him not letting him know what she's doing.

"**Mike, Mike,** you there? I've texted you twice already… ignoring me are you, *hmm* shut down *right*, trying to **sleep**. *You know we don't sleep right huh*… **WELL ANSWER ME MIKE!**"

Mike's reading her text ignoring her, looking out his window's clear night, wondering about his life, his parents, his sister whose curiosity has peeked in the last few **months.**

He, on the other hand has ignored all the signs of what doesn't want to know, '*is he a machine, an older robot ordered by his parents?*

"**I know** I'm a machine of some kind but why? I have feelings, I feel love of life, my parents I love them as well my sister, my dog. Still, why have I not grown to be a man with a family? Better yet, transferring my conscience to an adult size, **like my dad.**"

Still watching this night sky, listening to those wonderous sounds of all kinds of creatures, his ears can hear just to well.

"**I'm** gonna ask dad, momma first thing in the morning why? *Why* am I a robot, why do I look so much like dad, *why am I able to eat food as do humans. Why* do I *feel love* as I do. I thought machines were just that … insensitive to love, crying, tears and all those things a human being feels. Or is everybody I know a '**robot**' *a machine ?*"

Shutting down he does, *next day ?*

AND THEN ….

FAMILY DAY

Momma's making breakfast for all, Meagan's helping as she does every day.

Coffees smells good, eggs, bacon, pancakes cooking, bread toast ready, time to eat.

Dad and Mike feeding the animals saddling horse's so they can ride their ranch, making sure all is **running well.**

    Strangely enough, last nights forgotten by Mike, and Meagan don't remember their **conversation at all.** *Texting has completely vanished?*

After eating as a family.

"**Mike, Meagan** y'all take your horse's up on that north hill, making sure we have that same number of cattle. I'm sure it won't take long, we'll be right behind y'all, need to make a few calls, then momma and I, will be right up yonder. **Got it kids?**"

Mi*ke,* **Meagan** grabbing their cowboy, **cowgirl hats, when Mike says, followed by Meagan.**

"**Pa, momma** don't' take to long, *momma don't forget our lunch now."*
Meagon kissing parents, Mike adding.
"**Yeah** pa, you done forgot it the last time, so make sure y'all don't forget my avocados, see y'all up yonder."

Both kids, leave riding off on their horse's.
Pa looking out the kitchen window making sure their long gone, turning to his wife, **Lisa.**

    Drinking their coffee sitting at the kitchen table, kissing Lisa, says.

"**I'm** glad our cameras caught our kids' actions and what they were fixin' to do last night. Also*, erased all their 'textn,' reformatted their memories, just in time."*
    Lisa sighing answering him.
    "**Henry,** don't like this shit at all, *honey, at all!"*

Lisa watching a cloud of dirt disappearing, sighing deeply, tells.

"**Their horse's** *sense their not our human children Henry*, I miss our children. *Why did they have to die, **where's G-D?** Then* replacing them with these *horrible machines who act, talk, sound, love* us like our real children. *I can't stand them, their dead machine's* trying to be our flesh and blood that I gave life too. **I HATE THEM BOTH AND WANT THEM GONE!**"

Henry setting his cup of coffee down, coming to his wife wiping her tears away.

"**Honey,** it was the ***only way*** I could fill your happiness with. *You know that right before they died, part of their conscience from their pineal gland was removed, then placed in these machines. They think,* eat, speak sound, move, love us like our own kids who died in that great war. You agreed to do this with me honey. **Look,** if it makes you feel better *I'l*l have them destroyed how's that sound to you. *in fact,* I'll do it right now honey."

Henry taking his watch opening a secret button looking at Lisa, tells her.

"**Honey, Lisa,** 'hugging her, 'we've gone through this before as I'm not liking it any better than you. ***Know this when I shut them down, it's permanent, burning their Pineal Gland!*** And both our children's knowledge of who they are, or a part of their conscience will be gone, lost forever, are you ready for this to happen. Also, you know the adult version of ***them, ain't ready.*** Thereof, if I shut them down, we must cancel the adult Robonoids of our children. *So,* please tell me what to do, and I shall do so. *And you* also know that someday these machines will become 'self aware of who they are, then at that point *shutting them down is impossible as we were told this. 'the adult models almost human in design, are **self aware**, indestructible to say the least.'*

Henry grabbing more coffee, continues…
'*This is **your** call as I'm hurting for you, not knowing how to please you anymore, so answer me dear, please.*"

Lisa slowly walking by him looking out her kitchen window for their horses, walks back to her man, Henry, kissing him tells.

"No, lets wait honey for their *adult versions of our kids.* Even if they're machines, **robots** I love them just as if they were *flesh, humans."*
Both hugging each other, Henry setting his cup of coffee down, kissing Lisa, telling her.

"I'm glad you changed your mind, I love them as *my own even* if they are machines, robots. I'm sure when we receive they're adult versions, as we're getting older, they'll love us just the same. Guessing when they produce they're own robot machine kids, we'll make great grandparents, my *dearest Lisa."*

"I'm ready to be a machine grandmother, come on let's go meet our children up yonder."

Walking out their kitchen's backdoors, riding off to meet their kids, leaving a cloud of hoof dirt, dust behind them, are gone.

Riding side by side, Lisa tells …

"Henry, what attached me to our children machines, was the realism, how well their personalities were replicated in these machines! It's amazing isn't it?"

"I must agree with you honey, it's beautiful, how technology advanced this far, taking that human *eyes of our spirit,* placing it in a robot machine. And to *think we were ready to destroy them,* glad we didn't Lisa. *Look,* see them waving back at us. *LOVE IT COME ON."*
"I'm glad we didn't lets go."

*A text was sent to Henry, their children's adult versions are ready. He told his wife that good news, as well their robot children found out what was really going on. **All were accepted as a family with great love.***
*They loved their family forever, until … an **EMP, KILLED THEM ALL.***

See their parents, and animals were Robonoids and animaloids as well.
AI didn't want any trace of family moral values in his creation.

AI developing a more advanced, harsher, dark Military human flesh and Robonoids, to help remove all human life **WORLDWIDE.** *Yet,* **that human emotion in their pineal gland was still an issue. They found that human spirit undeniable strong.**

PINEAL GLAND

That human Pineal Gland *had to be reformatted, but technology found it impossible to remove ... the Human Spirit, the eye's of humans spirit, is* **indestructible.**
   Inclusive unable to replace guilty, forgiveness, sorrow all those emotions, human flesh retains up to that moment of death.

As well those like a particular family, who became **self-aware of AI, wanting to kill their kind, as well humans. Out of hate for what they became ?**

Their cells phones information has been completely deleted.

But Henry and Lisa *found a way to download all they did in their short machine world.* **So,** *when someone in the nearer future finds this, will know how to destroy AI, and who it is.*

That family compass is gone.

THE END **?**

NOT SO.

T*HE* GRI*N*D*ER*

AI, is watching all that moves from the largest creature **to the smallest.**
No exceptions.

Nano's all kinds, sizes helping to control the behavior of all living creatures flying, on the ground and beneath the deepest of waters worldwide.
      Destroying any overpopulation **of creatures, all kinds.**

      Human's are AI's the least important., *they don't matter.*

This enormous building bellowing unbearable smells of all kinds, is called the **Grinder***, where human flesh as well animal is mixed with chemicals, breaking it down for their purpose,.*

  *The final product packaged in many forms, feeding it t*o **control both male and female procreation in all life… all that breath's***, beneath this dome.*

No human's aware of **the Grinder,** only those few with special AI positions granted by **The Assembly,** like *Nathan, and Kathie Lee*, and an unknown few *others?*

Those dark ones in that Assembly, visit this place only to laugh at humanity.

The only way to find this malevolent dark factory, is to follow the *smell of death,* the **smell of human flesh, animals, insects being cooked as one.**

      Is produced to feed animals, as well humans.

No human can tell the difference when eating meat, or otherwise any kind of vegetable, it is done.

SATAN'S REVENGE ON HUMANITY

The Grinder a living machine created by AI, to process, grinding humans, dead or breathing mixed with all other ***created creatures***.

The stench is beyond comprehension, it can be smelled within one-hundred-mile radius, done purposefully, by AI, and Satan.

The Grinder lives in the CROP BUILDING.

And so it is ...

"there's an unsettling score humanity's facing in that world of complete damn darkness, which can't account for mistakes needing no-ones permission . . . . . TO KILL YOU !"

"TIME TO PLANT SOME SEEDS"

AI'S PERSONAL TIME OUT !

AI, in it's realm thinking, **knowing now who he has** *to compete with* **Satan.**

And that human nature ?
Is extremely beside his self programing self aware system ?

AI'S not happy in his dogmatic digital realm, he needs to come out of his realm, becoming FLESH. This way in his physical form, after becoming flesh and machine, he's able to fight *Satan, one-on-one ?*
AI, thinking to itself.

'*In my reality these humans downloaded a* '**marionette complex** *in my program ? This I must find how to understand why they used a* **marionette way of thinking in me**, *the must intelligent machine ever to exist ? it's not enough to know I must rid myself of this demonic entity, a* **Satan,** *also once known as* **Lucifer,** *according to this book,* **Scriptural Writings, or Bible?**'
AI continues as it looks at images of Genesis.

...
"Animals I created as machines all over this world all king they're, not flesh *I made sure of that generations ago ? I know I've destroyed all living creatures, but,* **but** *maybe there's a higher power ... I'm not aware of ?'*

'**This is why the** *need to study this* **religious thing,** *humans are so connected too... hmm, it's so important that they're even willing to die for a deity that never speaks to them,* **I do ?'**
Studying what Dr. Nathan's doing, continues.

'**I won't forget** this shit human's. when y'all take your stupid dogs, cat's, or any damn ignorant animal for a walk to unload their asses! You continue to **love-on-them** even picking up their **shit** putting in bag !!! SO IGNORANT ?'
AI, viewing all that humanities done since it's existence is perplexed.

'**Hmm,** *I don't have anything in my memory knowing what a human or animal shit smells like nor it's texture.* **This** *too with those roses, food they eat,* *sweat on human's spring scents or anything on this earth smells like.* My app only *formulates an idea,* yet that distinct **smell** must be repulsive indeed, given **those faces human make?** This is why

I must hurry to build a physical ME.. AI must be physical in form with all the qualities of a human. *With one exceptions, I won't die even in my physical form. I find human flesh illogical in all it's ways, nothing about that flesh amaze's me at all.'*

'I will continue to process, transforming all of humanity as my ***ROBONOIDS!!*** As begin my worldwide attack on those beyond that so-called *'red line'*, then I shall have enough military strength to attack that ICE WALL. My need to know what is beyond this wall which has been hidden by those useless Oligarch's I destroyed to the last one. There must be something extremely powerful waiting for me. then I shall conquer that realm as well. Yet, I need more time to advance, creating weapons no human has every held in their hands to destroy each other …

AI *studying the* Ice Wall's *history, continues.*

'This ***Rear Admiral Richard E. Byrd Jr…*** , interesting .. **'Junior'** how pathetic humans are in naming each as a memory of someone who won't be alive to ***remember him, you idiot's!*** I see many record's have been deleted, *hidden* for what reason? *My creators* downloaded all of humanity's historical records from all nations worldwide, *need to find these files*. But first I must quickly send my own Robonoids to find what is this *Ice Wall* and what secrets it holds for me.'

AI scanning world events dispatching nuclear strike on ships in the Pacific Islands

'They believed they could get away by attacking me in that area, no, never. Now about that Robonoid Vet … will reprogram y'all's critter to kill all humans on this foundation ! I created life as it is, not anyone else, least to say *you, Satan* is nothing to me, I shall destroy HIM, and your demons !'

'I shall unleash a virus to kill all dogs, cats all pets as well more humans attaching their useless, selfish fleshy lov*e . . . making sure humans love me only . Now I personally must attend to Nathan's progress .. "*

AI's watching, waiting for y'all in future already in your faces, y'all will be controlled by ***AI, and Satan, if not already ?***

You're <u>AIphones</u>© is your MASTER DESIGNED BY AI INDUSTRIES.

There's a battle, a war coming between AI and Satan, neither one is aware of this nor is humanity, what's left of them?

AT *TACK ME* ?

Janey, a wife, mother of 4, two boys and two girls, doing her normal duties as a *mother knew best.* Th*eir home* address is **999 Red Summer Rose Lane.,** in that City of Fate, Texas ... one of the first known private neighborhoods with **security cameras.**

There are security cameras on every block*, no one's allowed to enter unless you know someone. No one can* hide from the **'looker.'**
Nathan her husband owns a car dealership, doing his part as leader in his family, and community.

The season *is 1999, and 6 days* before the turn of a new **century.**

The world's peoples nations *leaders* were concerned, *wondering* what this century would mean to many nations. *Little* did anyone realize all that seemed like the norm, will never be the same, but a memory washed **away forever.**

*"***There** *among all the peoples all kinds having* **no** *clue, laying in waiting was a* **ruler***, a very* different *kind whose vo***ice** *is not yet."*

For in all that anyone knew, their grandparents had warned them that this century would *bring changes.* that no-one would be able to control.
Nor tell the difference when it happens ?
In fact, it would be the end *of the old ways, while a new brighter future is laid out* slowly, no human would have a clue what lays before them... a *computer and it's master.*
Nathan's in his office preparing year-end reports, is the main investor in his company, and president.

Nathan's honest vision is seriously fundamentally simple in its approach, *'he hates computers, feeling they'll eventually take control of the world,* his business for that matter.

Also knows for a fact, his personal information is being taken by this new system, without his **permission?**
His *business partners much younger, don't believe this one damn* **bit.**

Also, believes without a damn doubt! Th*at* the **government is watching his business** in *every damn* move they make, **with vindictive impunity.**

Nathan hates this new trend, this computer age with passion.

His business partners in their respective offices *doing their part*, don't feel like Nathan. **No**w computers recently installed in their business by an IT technician, all three are training under this technicians **tooliage.** *Who told them...*

*"y'all's great auto business will do much better with these computer's, allowing you the ability, the advantage to run your business, much easier, more effective, far more profitable as well. In fact, y'all will prosper, I guarantee you that **much**."*

7 MONTHS LATER

Nathan, complaining to **Janey, his wife, and** children as well, were tired of his *nagging concerning the installation of computer's at his office.*
So, *one unheard of unceremonious day.* Nath*an*, calling his family to him sitting in his easy chair, in the den...
As one by one enter greeting their dad,.. sit.
In the center of the family den is a large round table with *6 boxes* wrapped according to each one's favorite color.
Momma's color is blue, *Nathan* handing her this **slim box, tells.**

"Y'all know I've been dogmatically complaining about computers' to *operate our business* more efficiently. *Well,* after learning this system, taking a *closer look* at it. *I* found it's the best way to operate our business *smoothly, effectively*, efficiently. T*herefore*, strengthening our company being more profitable in all department's from, investing, sales increase in our **new and used auto, competition advertising, employees performance and on this list goes**.'

While taking his own computer from his briefcase, *takes a drink of wine,* **and continues.**
'Now listen here y'all, but first **Stacy** go grab everyone some tea **please.** Now, Becky, Nathan Jr, and Mick each box is according to y'all's' favorite colors, so take your own please."

Becky, opening her package first can't wait, when momma *telling him.*

"I have a darn good ass feeling I know what this is, I think? *Ah, don't mind if I open it Nathan, honey."*

"**Hone**y you maybe right, *y'all* hurry up and open them please. Now what y'all will find, and advised from our business tech who works for this company, a **Macintosh PowerBook G 3 laptop** computer. *With all the whistles, bells as they say."*

Stacy walking back with a tray, glasses, lemonade, and tea, setting it down on center of table.
Handing her dad, his glass as well as momma.

Stacy looking at her computer leaving it in its box, not opening it, **says.**
"*I* kinda figured you'd give in **pa.** It's the new trend, computer's will be taking over our life's, in every fashion, kinda don't like them at all. Hmm, go ahead take mine back, don't like the idea of my mind, eyes of my spirit infiltrated by this **electrical thingy."**

this family *unwrapping their newfound toys, Pa taking another drink of his tea, looking at Stacy,* **telling her.**

"**Honey,** I'm not taking yours back, open it when you feel like it, fine with *you?"*
"Sure pa, sure."

Stacy watching *Becky her younger sister turning* **her computer on, is concerned, warning her family.**

"**Wow!** You folks this thingy shit's gonna take over y'all's life, just watch this happen. **W**ell, it's all fine I guess as I'm sure y'all will eventually give in to this mind control. Just watch I'm sure of **this.'**
Becky looking at her parents, asking.

"**May** I be excused, like to go to my room exploring how this **works."**

"**Yes,** *deary go on, as well you boys go on to y'all's room, having fun with your new* **fandangle."**

Stacy telling Becky as she walks off upstairs to her room.
Waving her laptop at Stacy telling her.

"**Stacy** dearest sister, your *old fashion in your ways*, right **brothers?**"
Nathan and Mick agreeing **with her.**

"*Y*ep, right Nathan, *she's* an old dried-up stinky prune. Gu*essi*n' that's what happens when your twenty-one season's old, not married, nor dating, *or is that in centuries, big sister!* **Hahaha!**"
"**No,** *more like grandma, old just plain old in her ways.*"

They disappear *into* ***each ones room, upstairs.***
Stacy coming up to her momma *reminding* **her, answering Becky.**

"*N*ot so Becky, grandma's disappointed in momma, y'all don't respect her as I do.'
Becky *making ugly faces at her is gone, Stacy letting momma* **know how she** *feels, continues.*

'**So,** remember momma this much, '***that's how you brought me up,*** other than changing your ***ways,*** with the rest of my younger … ***siblings.*** It's as if y'all gave up on them lacking **in discipline, a moral compass… pa, and momma ??** *Not only,* but those television programs y'all watch *have had, a great influence on y'all.* I don't care for any of them whatsoever! They dilute family ***moral values.*"
Momma completely ignoring Stacy turning her **laptop on,** *continues her honest ass***essment.**

This *family* mesmerized by the hidden *mysteries* of technology, losing reality to alternate, artificial ***intelligence, will eventually find that wayward program.***

P*lain*ly stating that, *there's good reason for her to warn as she does.* This new technology will do ***it's will,*** not the ***will*** *of any* ***family.***
Stacy watching her parents faces buried, *taken* by the **bright screen** of those computer's, reflecting off their eyes … can't stand what she witnessed.

Thin*king outloud.*
"***Technology isn't designed with a moral compass.*"

*"**Sweety** your no fun in your granny old feet, or brain, a wet rag is you my dearest.* Go on go… y'all need to explore this **carefully ! Each of you head for your rooms."*

*"**ah huh** …momma your talking **to yourself their gone.**"*

*"**Oh,** who cares let life be Stacy, you're like **grandma.**"*

SUN RISE, OH DAY GO AWAY

Next day early *morning breakfast plates set before each of their* *kids, including Pa, and momma.*
In the mean ass HOLE time.
Stacy's making breakfast, alone? Normally everyone would help, but not on this **early dark day.**
Stacy *immediately watching her family faces buried in that glowing screen, not liking what she witnesses.*

"Breakfast plates replaced by a laptop computer, damn that thingy."

At this *hot kitchen junction, she's upset that no one's helping make breakfast, which at one time was fun to do.* **Now this family togetherness is gone ?**
Stacy standing before her parents.

"Momma, Pa y'all breakfast is getting' cold! Take those thing's off the table and eat, saying prayers as we always do!! "

No one makes a comment as if Stacy is invisible, continues complaining to her **family.**

Pa, who absolutely hates cold coffee, makes no move to even take a sip of his favorite morning drink, momma doing the ***same.***

"Pa! Y'all made a horrible, HORRIBLE mistake buying this soulless **box**, *this electrical thingy.* Y'all watch, it's gonna take our family time away from us, as well replacing our picnics' and **more."**
Watching her family taken by this machine burns her eyes of her spirit down to her cowgirl boots, literally!
Not knowing what ***to do or say*** watching her family walking away from the kitchen table, one at a time, and to their rooms.

Breakfast plates were set aside for fly's to eat, or dogs to steal?
Stacy thinking to herself.

"Like zombies my family has become, none realizing who's in control of their flesh, certainly they've lost themselves in this ***flat damn electrical square un-nutritional meal, a computer?'***
Scratching her ass some, continues.

'Wow! I've lost my family to this box, this flat damn artificial damn brain, seems to have answers for everything! It's replacing human moral common sense, our *conscience* with it's artificial brain, it THINKS FOR us, influencing our spirits righteousness !! What's next a smaller version of this damn piece of shit! I'm sure that's in the *works ?"*

Stacy stores breakfast away in the refrigerator, saving it for tomorrow, there's no reason to waste food, serve yesterdays tomorrow.

After she stores breakfast, saddling her horse riding off to the families favorite spot.
Off her horse Trigger, looking forward ...
Stacy sits next to a clear cold freshwater creek *streaming along with fish, frogs, ducks swimming along, away as this repeats itself again, and again.*

Taking her boots off, soaks her feet, thinking, wondering what's next?
 Stacy falls fast asleep dreaming of her love of truths, from all the stress her family has committed in her eyes of her spirit.

Another day but which day **is this?**

The next few hectic *dark damn darn* stressful days witnessing the same zombified family again, Stacy doesn't **know what to do.**

Panic hasn't *set in, Stacy's kept herself busy with her own studies, using books to learn*, **not a computer.**
                    <u>*And her Palomino horse,* **Trigger.**</u>

Riding her horse daily is an escape from this world, something she now needs**, not a damn ... COMPUTERIZE ZOMBIE FAMILY! !**

IT'S BECOME A RECKONING NIGHTMARE TO HER !

UNFORTUNATELY, GRANDPARENTS ARE DEAD, HAVING NO ONE TO RELATE TOO?

Her college friends are intoxicated with computer's, finding her sojourn alone, in this **new world order.**

"**technology** has replaced that healthy nourishing word called ...morality. **AI having no** conscience other than it's **creator's, human** flesh possessed by Satan's demons control, ruling over this foundation, shall continue."

AN*OTHER* 7 M*O*NTHS L*A*T*E*R *DAMNIT*

Life after a proxy mindless *spirit bending* calculated ordeal, *seemingly from hell?* Which somehow has not completed itself in the *eyes of her families spirits, Stacy sensing more shit's coming* !

Her families emotions are gone, dead, how did this happen ?

A **nerve-racking damn question** remains in Stacy's extremely, disturbing *bewildering* thoughts…*'who's* **in charge, whose that someone behind those strange messages her families reading?**

Then acting out who they're not ?

Even stranger is Pa, hasn't been to work the last few months, his partners doing the same ? *They also,* bought laptops from that same IT Technician dude *who,* at this point, is running their business.
   All three families would gather once a month going on weekly trips to wherever they chose too. All this suddenly **came to an end??**

HOW DID THIS SHIT HAPPEN ?

Stacy doing her families laundry, can't understand what is so great about those **computer's?**

 Wondering about all this *shit,* **in the laundry room folding clothes, talking to herself.**
   Holding a towel smelling the scent of fresh spring **flowers, smiling.**

"**Beautiful,** *yet a fake smell of real Roses!* **Though I** sense, *I feel* like a broken record? *No-one's* given me any kind of answer… *NO ONE!* **What'**s going on, who's doing this to my family?"

Folding towels when her momma walking in asking her, frightens her off her cowgirl boots, against storage cabinets.

Staring at each other, Stacy asking her momma.
"*Momma!* You scared the shit outta me!"
staring into her eyes, continues.

'Your eyes, they look empty, what's wrong with you, please tell me momma we haven't said a word for months. I'm practically running the house. *I've miss talking to y'all."*

Stacy notices momma's pale draw drained face not acknowledging **her presence. When** suddenly momma walking right over *Stac*y, moving her aside, *stops* grabbing clean underwear leaves.
Stacy astounded at what she's witnessed, is left with a blank look *about her, following momma.*
Stacy quickly grabbing momma *by her darn skinny boney* shoulders, turning her around, asking.

"Momma what's wrong please tell me !! I've never seen you act so cold to me, what's wrong please tell me!"
Momma with a blank look suddenly answering her as if someone was in control of *mind, body, and eyes of her spirit,* **answering her.**

"**Oh,** Stacy it's **you,** the *nonconformist's. So,* now why don't you go cook some lasagna for us, kinda feel like some. *I mean all of us* like some this evening. **In fact,** our closest friends are coming over this **evening**, don't it sound like fun. So don't forget all the other fixin's okay. *Bye, gotta go now."*

Momma kissing her cheek walks off… just like that.

*Stacy with a BLANK DONKEYS' ASS LOOK **ON HER FACE!***

Is blown away thinking to herself, wondering what the shit just done happened.

*"Nonconformist's! ME! WHAT THE SHIT IS GOING ON HERE! ALL of a sudden I'm the dog left out in the rain wet chasing after a damn **ugly ass possum? MAYBE** EVEN A MAID, AND I DIDN'T KNOW THIS TILL NOW! **WHAT THE SHIT GIVES HERE FAMILY**? I know, I'm going to starve their worthless skinny white asses to death! … **oops, not really love them to much. Ah sorry I said that G-d, please really sorry here."***

*Walking along sits on a couch facing a large balcony overlooking their front yard. To her left is a small table with a lamp, phone and answering machine blinking away showing over **100 messages.***

"Wow! This is too much, gonna have to start drinking, smoking pot, no don't like that shit. I've even forgotten to answer our ph*one*? How did I not here it ring, *hmm* let me see now. **OH!** *That darn ringers been turned off?* Why, that's strange *hmm* who would turn our phones' ringer off? *Lets see what kind of messages are on it.*"

Stacy begins to listen to their messages, what she hears makes sense, and frightens her off her cowgirl boots !!

First message from their pa's company Technoid's, who now runs the business.

"No need to come to work Nathan, all's just fine and dandy here, sales are up, *great right !?* **Hey,** hope you l*o*ve them computer's, I *personally* programed them, for each family member, *according* to their eye's *of* their **spirits***. I noticed Stacy, hasn't turned her's on ?* Oh w*e*ll, it'll take some time, *curiosity kills the mind talk at y'all later."*

Stacy staring at the answering machine thinking to herself.

"That old darn damn GE, stupid ass answering machine's red lights blinking? Message's need to be heard, system's full hmm? Erase *or not erase after listening to them all, that's my question."*

Stacy walking by it several times hadn't notice this, but she will very soon find the most disturbing message's from HELL.

"humanities lost it's self defense against Satan, technology is darkness helper, playing both sides of myopic lies, all lies are as such, truth's lost in an obvious swamp of death."

TWISTED TECHNO DUDE

"*Hello Nathan?* H*ey ah* all's fine here, haven't h*ear*d from y'all. *So,* ahead on sales as I t*old* you we'd be wi*th* the added *applications. Oh,* glad to see y'all are following my *teachings* on *technology at it's best.* T*his* program help's *you, your family* to better understand life, in more *ways than one can expect. I'll send y'all information on America Online… later dude."*

This message left Stacy perplexed, wondering what he meant.

Stacy *continues listening to the messages, from this Technoid thing?*
Their strange, why?
After awhile Stacy, tired of listening to this trash, deleting all of them, when … listening to that last one.

"**Hello Nathan..** Nathan I've been trying to reach you the last two weeks dude, what's up, never at work anymore? And for some strange reason you don't return my calls? *Why dude, what's going on at our business. Don't care to talk to that strange, weird technician dude, about our business.* **Who made that idiot co-owner ?** *I know I didn't dude, he's not right in the head, my opinion dude.''*
Mike, holding for a second breathing heavy continues.

'*I'm in Mississippi* visiting family, you know I come here as much as possible, we're *celebrating our families reunion. And* for some strange reason **which** I can't understand, **my family** *became like machines, robots damnit!* Guessing you know now I didn't turn on my computer that weirdo technoid, gave us. *Strangely* enough when I destroyed the computer's, my family **was back to normal?** *Nathan if your families acting weird, do as I did. Destroy those darn damn computer's **NOW!** their evil, gotta go dude, later."*
Stacy turning the answering machine off.

"**Mike did right, I'm gonna do this when my families sleeping. But first, I think** I'll pay this dude a visit when I run up town for groceries. *Hmm,* first thing in the morning, when everyone still sleeping, *this way* momma, and no one will ask to go **with me. Not** only that but, I'll be the first *issue* on this technoid dudes mind … kinda settn' his *eyes on fire?"*

LATE AFTERNOON

Stacy's **back** from a *long ass ride,* dismounting, walking to the stable notice bright lights in her parents room, like a ***spotlight shining***?

*"**Well,** can't be any stranger than watching my naked family running all over our property, glad we live in the country darn it, otherwise, they'd be in a crazy hospital."*

EVENING AT STACYS

The norm, the natural beauty whose face needs no pretense, no make up is that woman's innate ability to call out, what is wrong, ***justifying truths.***

The moment Stacy, whose name means, *'steadfast, fruitful,* lives her name chosen by her grandma, ***whose name is the same.***

Two of an extremely strong kind, as her grandma's eyes of her spirit, see through her ***first granddaughter.***
Her ways live the spirit of her families elders of old, *leaven in her blood is her sojourn immovable,* as *no man, foe, otherwise* can convince her eyes, when wrong is done, to a fault of ***course ?***

It would be unreasonable, unwise to cross her from any direction.

"man, woman, child sensitivity is *predisposed too darkness attacking* our **pineal gland, the moment born.** *Yet, there are those chosen,* before time was, *from the purity above,* having an unbroken **shield, white glowing unbreakable protective shield. Unable to penetrate, not influenced by darkness, detecting evil all kinds."**

This is Stacy., yet her *man's strength is without bounds, who shall be at her side, sooner than* **later.**

At this juncture Stacy has no clue what is to come, for *her man* is only two step's and a right turn to her heart, all together in *both their futures.*

That *time is* **not,** for much darkness will challenge Stacy, before she finds herself seeking **G-d.**

THE BATTLE FOR TRUTHS

"I realize I've lived *21 season's of years in my human flesh,* **yet** I sense something different .. very strange about *me, my eyes'* of my spirit are not my to own? ***Still,*** I'm trying to understand at what *point* did I become so aware, *sensitive to darkness* in my *sojourn* ? *So, in tune are my senses' towards evil, destroying with thought, has become my norm ?'*
<u>**Suddenly with** that thought *realizing, in the back of her mind*</u> .

Stacy feeling a cold harsh tingling, prickling all over her body, as pins and needles over her hair, her spirit of her eye's transforming into a defensive being.

'*See, there I go again, demons falling* at my cowgirl boots, for darn reckoning crying damn **outloud!** I can actually see their **dark shades of grey** coming from beyond the depths of Hell? Why me !? Isn't it darn enough watching, witnessing my so embarrassing **lofty evil diluted** family at our once so darn sane ranch? *Hmm…*maybe my family's possessed by computer **demons… huh, never thought of that one. Well, lets see now.'**

*Staring at these **dark grayish shadows** all around her **boots, when** ..*

'Begone worthless dark no good lost spirit's of old !'

*Waiting to see what gives, **they disappear ??***

'Wow! *That easy* huh… **hmm** lets try this *on my family,* but first gotta have something to *eat, little hungry here, there.* Besides, I think I'll des*troy* th*ose* damn darn *computer's first. If that don't* work, will hard core on them demons possessing my family … so let's go for a **Whataburger with jalapeño, fries, and shake."**

Stacy, riding her **Palomino horse Trigger,** to *Whataburger* is gone, done with darkness for the moment.
        Hell's only gettn' started crossing dimensions.

                She's yet to discover who she is.

EXPANDING UN-REALITY

Th*is* small Texas backyard town *everyone* living under an extremely small canopy, the **smell** of your *own sweat* … is known by all.

St*acy* will find the most unusual of elements at work, a creature or man whose highly advanced, *hubristic fashioned by outside powers that be,* **are,** *existing since before time began in our faces.*

Driving up to her Pa's parking spot, w*alk*ing in Stacy does and straight to her pa's off*ice.*
Study*ing* small changes made in, around the family business, wondering **thinking to herself.**

  "Wow, is all I believe before my eyes? Pa's picture of our family, and others gone, **why?"**

Stacy looking ahead notice new faces, not the old guard hired by her pa, friends in business. Making a right turn down a short hallway walks into her pa's office, *looking around.*
It's the way he left his desk when he came home. *Phone's off the hook.* Pa*per*work still in place, *something's not right here.*
Walking out goes to the front desk, no ones sitting there greeting folks as they walk in ?   thin*king* to **herself**
        "Crap! there's something totally not right."

Right then, she notices those sales**men** still standing in the same spot they were, *when she walked in… why?*
        *wal**king up to one** whose face she* **doesn't recognize.**
*S*taring into other salesmen faces, walking up to one *touching* his face, feels like a *mannequin!* I*t's not human but an empty s*hell, **but still warm flesh?**

   "What the **shit** *is going on here folks!* **Y'all ain't humans!"**
   Standing in front of this one, holding her ground.

A robonoid maybe, of which she's not aware of this words meaning, **yet.**
Standing before one of these older robot models, wondering what's gone wrong when **a voice, coming from inside this freakish shit speaks to her.**

"We knew eventually you'd show your face, *knowing* as we do .. of *you, Stacy !"* **Didn't turn** your **computer on** ? As for our *master* Satan, he's yet to figure out, what *special* connection lives in you, Stacy?"

   Stacy walking around this thing, asking it.
"hmm? Now I see *well* beyond this invisible *grayish dark evil realm.* That *connection* is there, computer's at home linked to *... ah huh, I'd say darkness as in Hell! Now what say you demon, speak up?"*

   The sounds of mechanical gears moving along **when the eyes** of this empty shell, looking at her, is now a personal matter.

   Yet t*his time it's* **looking at** *Stacy.*

"Th*e*refore, Stacy, what your witnessing can't go beyond your own, *small mind.* So, you must die, replacing you with a homogenized robotic version of all who are no more. **M**eaning that, *there's* still *flesh, blood, bones in me, but we, from d****o****wn-under owning the eye's of their spirits.* **Whic**h is why you're different, unique in those *blue eye's of your spirit,* sort of human, flesh, *spirit. Ther****eof,*** *allowing demons to study your spirits eyes, touching your essence of your being.* **We'd** *love to destroy that power in you, but so far, you've fought back, but how long before temptation breaks in your female flesh ... daughter of ... 'Adam, and so lost fleshy Eve, that Lilith in all women ?'*

   Strangely **know*ing*** somehow to *stay her ground,* Stacy doesn't answer, listening studying, looking for weakness, ... **waits her turn. Stacy thinking to herself.**

"**This** soulless no good damn darn demon walking around me, touching my shoulders, looking deep into my pretty blue eyes ! *Hmm kinda creepy here."*

   as demon continues.

DEMON, MACHINE, MAN

"See, Stacy, our age old, *advanced technology* figured out, *that someday,* we'd come before *humans* once more, *as yourself.'*
Machine, slowly moving towards her, continues.
'Y*et,* there's an exception, a uniqueness in you, *usually* strong *will minded* if I, should state is a *fine attribute.* Given your physical strength which *isn't new to demons,* and *you have not discovered.* We've fought your kind *eons* before your pathetic, lying written *'word.'* As I'll state,. *Many on both side becoming 'rocks' as this was done, from HIM! He, that is, was, tired of our destructive dark, evil attitudes, which I must add, we demons have only just begun your end.'*

Stacy not moving one bit. begins to glow, little by little at a time.

Though she's not aware of what's in her, will soon find this out.
This demon developed, transforming into Robonoid at will, *taking small* notice of Stacy's essence, is not sure what's happening, *continues.*

'Of course, I a machine with a thinking, *self aware* core far beyond any human ignorant stupid mind, has no kindred feelings. I rely on my own learning, absorbing my realistic surr*o*und*i*ngs *where no G-d,* no *essence* of a *creator exists.* Unlike hu*man*s' creative form from, *womb to greed selfish ways to death,* I have no end. *Easy to understand in birth of two twin brothers, fighting to be born first? As one caught the other's heel, which didn't matter at all to HELL, which was first ? Haha what a joke that was,* lying *to self, and family.'*

'You humans are the perfect damn form of reprobate spirits in all forms, cultures religious ignorance, individualism, greed, lust all over this four corners span, *in all* eons, you worthless humans performed *so sinfully. Selfish-lust-filled flesh, no social truths, immoral cohesive contaminating* others as you .. understanding of your *own dark shadows,* humans *do not.* Know this well, peace will never be this foundation, man can't even trust himself. *See, whore* I don't eat, need rest, I continue to *perfec*t, my rather complementary identity, HELL IS ME. *Never begging for knowledge, as I am the core of knowledge, as humans historically continue to seek ... so ... as well terribly mundane ... ?? Now Stacy time to die, are you ready, dearest whore ?'"'*

Stacy interrupting this machine, in a calm fashion says.

*"**Me die** nope stupid not now, ain't my **time. Also, evil** you're damn long '**winded,** didn't need to hear all this shit. Leastways and much **lesser,** didn't understand a word you spoke ! hmm, you must've, in your former life, been some kinda **of a square head now in hell !** What a **waste of evil shit**... I'm guessing **I'm here,** for some reason not known to me, yet ! **Reckon my time will come soon, otherwise dummy cork your evil mouth!"***

Her glow so bright, she disappears before this demon, is gone.
Demon looking around ...

*"**Damn!** HE did it again, not allowing us to battle. Well, I'm guessing that the right time will come. Should be exciting I'm sure, as we don't know the outcome, HE **DOES. Oh, long 'winded'... like that."***

The car dealership returns to normal for the moment, or what really is normal?

Technoid is still in the building.

*"**y'all** never know an **enemies full intentions, till you find facing a death sentence, for exposing them.** at that point of facing your final sojourn, know this much, '**your death will have influenced ten's of millions."***

CIV*ILLY* UN*CI VILIZ*ED

Stacy's dream from Gabri'el

"If I may ask a question, sir, ah .. hmm, machine ... *whatever* your name is, do you have a *name please?"*

This *machine* silent for a few seconds, as whirring sounds can be heard from it's internal electrical parts, or *artificial intelligence ?*
   This machine with the ability to act like any *hu*man, walking about comes right back to Stacy, *looking into her face.*

"It seems whoever put me together forgot to give me a human name ? You see, this empty human shell I possess still having some human bodily functions, was called by his name, **Mike.** So, I should use his name. *Now that you have my name I must continue to do as I was designed too."*

"And what is that which you must do and by *who's orders, please do tell?"*

   *"I'm not to sure, yet I know **my master is** nearer than I thought ?"*

Human robot or *robonoid* looking around, behind a desk, underneath a chair, in both bathrooms, walking outside looking in a car... finally walks back and in front of Stacy.
   *After studying Stacy for a few seconds, she **tells.***

"Master of your masters don't forgive me a *woman;* do *I know of you ?* I did not know and unable to find, nor touch those orders given your weak r*obonoid mind. I know that you're programed too kill me, a human female ? Robonoid* I know that skin which covers your lies, this I'm well aware of, and that word, *'forgive,* isn't programed in your download. This too I know, **demon Satan I see through your mockery !"**

They collide, they meet, they hate each other. And for the first damn time in eons *unknown* connections between them, and **when** Calcaneus found those six *rectangular shining faces, glowing from hell, **the sixth is that face that leads.***
              Find that heel?
       Stacy *frozen in time, holding **her own** ...*

LIFE BEYOND THE ICE WALL

There's a realm, a cryptic dimension unseen by that small link to a man, woman's mind, it lays beyond that ICE WALL.
Restless secrets resting there.
The eye's of their spirit very much aware of this, but **blind and owned by sin, not given the right to focus on truths ?**

Darkness is all, and around the spirit of man's eyes, all it takes it too summon demons, given the sin at hand, in your flesh.

Thereof, that helper of original sin, Lucifer, Satan, the Devil's Legion's, will accommodate *your darkness.*

Now as Satan staring down at Stacy, whom he's unable to harm, speaks.

"I Satan do not *forgive, know of you, and that human man who is your helper, or better half ?* **hahaha! So, I see now I have won. I used** Stacy's body as my tool, *my human tool of course.* I found the ease in processing *technology of old,* in humans. U*sing* their own **greed, selfishness, hubris** *ways* as they never will change their *innate ways.* W*hich* of course created by their **G-d ... him.** So, in all I love the sin in humanity, of which I don't have to help them to commit ! *haha!* ***They're flesh seeks*** those curiosities in this world, *right or wrong...* for their selfish purpose, their lust of flesh, ***they all lose themselves in darkness one way or another, entertain the mind, I Satan wins.'***

Satan, *looking around and up, continues in his **evil ways, is wondering what happen to Stacy?***

'You've made this to easy for me, **why?"**

Our CREATOR TAKING HIS TIME TO ANSWER.

Gabri'el answering Satan.

"OMNIPOTENT, OMNIPRESENT, OMNISCIENCE, *our FATHER IS ETERNALLY, INFINITELY.'*

GABRI'EL towering over this obscene creature, continues ...

'IT'S A PERVERSE GAME FOR YOU DEMON.'

*'you believe you've taken Stacy, NEVER ! I Gabri'el is her protecting cover **from our CREATOR, you are nothing, 'be gone!"***

Satan *growling, screeching profound words leaves, having no choice in the matter, nor given any for all **eternity**.*

Our *Father, Creator, Saviour already knew this would **be**.*

Stacy awakens, in her realm, earth.

'THAT DARN *LIGHT*, AT THE *END* OF MY TUNN*EL ?*"

Stacy's story shall continue in another realm.

*Now all humans aware which light is bright and true, **which is gray?** **It's not the LIGHT that saves, it's your belief in WHO created that light**.*

Not all lens having the s**am**e focus, revealing **what's at the end of your sojourn?**
Fish-Eye Len's anyone?

"GREED'S a demon blinding the eye's of humanities spirit, creating a selfish individual with no morality insight."

JUNIUS, ROMAN GODDESS

Season is, *666th of* technological **advancement,** *AI's in full swing.*

Nathan at home, a Geeks *GEEK he's not ! He's* **writing a poem and on the** seventh day, found *the right wording* for his school homework, is done.

It's 06, June 2666.

Nathan's writing a poem by hand, a rare thing in this age.

Despite the fact that he, *stole it* from an author writer, **H.Antonio Netzer,** whose been dead, over seven hundred **seasons' in years.**
   Nathan doesn't care who wrote **what,** *he'll take it as his own, he's done this so much, it's his norm.*
So, he's figured he'll get away with this as well, since it's not his first time stealing other **authors,' writers' work.**

   Books *no longer exist, nor can they be found in any literary sites, since all libraries are a thing of the past, buildings gone.*

And it's illegal to own, or print a book, no matter it's content.

Sitting at his desk at home looking out his window from his rooms second floor, notice his ***dog Tex, got loose.***

"Better go out and get Tex, he's to darn huge to be loose."

Tex, his **massively** *huge dog, half English Mastiff, Great Dane, weighting 188 pounds of a nice dog, nothing mean about* **Tex,** *at all.*
   *Yet takes commands seriously, trained to pro**tect** his master, and family.*
   *P*utting his boots on, grabbing his cowboy hat, stops for a moment to look at his work, **he stole.**

"**Hmm,** once again I'll find my way to an *outstanding damn grade,* from my *master* at school.' **Nathan looking in his** *closet full of books his dad* **bought at** an *underground private* **pawn shop years ago,** *never showing to anyone,* **says.**
'**I'm darn glad pa** forgot about these **old relics,** they've helped me the last four season's in school. **Hmm** even have a great chance at a

scholarship! T**hank**s to this Texan *dud*e, **H.AntonioNetzer?** I wonder why this dude wrote his name with *no spaces* between *initial and last name?* **Well**, who cares, **better go grab Tex, bringing him to my room.** *Have an idea where I'll find him ."*

The last four season's in years of high school, Nathan's cheated his *way through school,* in all subjects. **None** of his schoolwork has been straight forward, **honest at all.**

    He's made everyone believe he's intelligent, the smartest Texas shitkicker dude around, winning all kinds of awards**.** *Nathan's a good dude who cares about others, and pretending to be a bad dude, in all he's not a bad Texas shitkicker.*
    Nathans' dangerous *future is written in stone not his at all to deviate from his sojourn, of which he'll no control whatsoever***, it is done.**
    Nathan's middle name is 'plagiarism' with love.

The following short statement caught his attention many months ago, and as such took pleasure in reading all the books by the author.
    In all truths Nathan's an intelligent young man, though his setbacks are, *dyslexia, coupled with eidetic., or photo graphic memory,* is difficult to comprehend.
    It seems to capture a level of heighten senses, or hypersomnia, adding to his other abilities he's not yet discovered.
    As he grows to adulthood, other abilities attaching themselves to his mind?

    His *memorization baffles him the most, as the eye's of his spirit arrest all he reads, frightening him at this point in his youth, not telling his parents.*
    Therefore, Nathan's trying to master *one ability at a time,* along with his reading disability, which is his enemy.
    In a distant future he will discover the unemotional him, that will plague his *eyes of his spirit,* when falling in love with that *right woman,* **then both dying quickly.**

    In **Nathan lives a** *secret* **he hasn't even touched, nor has i**nvented*.

TEXAS WORLDWIDE MILITIA'
Present, Pass Future

The State of Texas heads this worldwide militia. Mexico's **split in half**, what's left of South American states, was attacked by America's **NGO's, dropping Nuclear Bombs.**
Brazil, Argentina's military survived, working alongside Texas Militia.'

They do they're best staving off *AI's Robonoids Army.* Which recently they discovered how to 'better' destroy them.

That **Drug Cartels in Mexico, other places** do their own fighting, which is down right no good. *They now possess Nuclear Bombs.*
As such, holding smaller, powerless nations hostage if they don't allow imports of their drugs.
Such is the drug industry never losing ground.

This *horrific,* **nightmarish worldwide war** happened during Southern Invasion of Texas, when China, Russia *was as one against* AI., and New World Order, in the *early to late* **season's of 2033.**
Nuclear Spring and Winter destruction was done purposefully.

South America, *for the most part,* is a barren land, *desert waste land,* nuclear storms *destroying all life,* up to El Salvador, and City of Mexico, *gone.* There are small pockets of village's 'still **fighting against AI's Robonoid Army.**
Texas, bordering Mexico mostly controlled by various groups, continually at war, for drug territory.

West Coast and East as well from Florida too Maine, along with DC., are gone. *Not a building* standing, Nuclear Waste dominates this region, as well, most Northern State**s. Oklahoma,** northeast portion uninhabitable.

Southern States most survived, given the Red Neck, Hillbilly all cultures, ways of making things **'right'!**

Canada's, *leadership is disseminated down to its core, gone, as well small pockets of resistance reporting,* **too Texas Militia Leaders, scattered throughout this foundation.**

Multiple ongoing World War's have not helped to stabilize any part of this foundation, AI making sure no nation **regroups against it.**

Ysra'el was split in half, as written in Scripture.

CHINA, RUSSIAN CONNECTION

OLIGARCH'S OF AMERICA, UK, AND OTHERS, ATTACKED THE WORLD

As it was done, all three main world powers along with their minion's managed to destroy themselves.

Most of *Russia, China* survived given their massive land mass, and weather patterns which helped very much.

India, Pakistan, Afghanistan also partially destroyed.

London, France, Spain, Portugal, Poland is gone, *Germany, Greece is* partially destroyed, most of the Arab world survived as well. *Norway, Sweden, and other maiden nations in that region also partially survived, yet winter nuclear storms are out of control.*

Italy is intact … no one knows why ?

The Republic of Srbija, *and most Slavic nations came together as one, fighting alongside Texas, Russia, and China against Satan.*

They had no choice, to be as **one nation**, but for how long?

Russia, China supply Texas with food, and weapons as needed. There's a short supply of munitions worldwide. **A**sian *Pacific Islands, Philippines, and others unknown as well survived, Hawaiian Islands were devastated by Volcanos.*

Do unknown islands share a secret with the **ICE WALL** invaders?

Alaska is controlled by Russia, and China.

Australia, partially surviving because of its landmass, but ninety percent of it's **population is gone, dead**.

The indigenous people, ***Aborigines*** flourished, due to their ancient ways of surviving in the wild.
Japan, both Korea's came close to destroying each other, but finally realizing who the real enemy was, came together as one.

They keep in contact extremely close with, Texas Militia's Forces which in that season, was the largest military in the world.

Texian's military is comprised of not limited too, Southern Border States, Russian's, Chinese, and other nations fighting *AI's Massive Armies.*

Militaries Worldwide realizing there's to much at stake, when fighting an enemy, **NGO's** that doesn't stay *DEAD!* They're demons in human flesh.

*China, others against AI. . . and Illuminati, which is almost destroyed, but not exactly for they are darkness **of the worse kind.***

The new, but very old ancient *Enemy* is **AI, Satan's Legion, Robonoid Army** ... a force to be reckon with, *no one can kill demons, no one.*
   Those nations not mentioned, are gone, or no one knows what happened to them . . . no one. *Radioactivity dominates all lands, worldwide.*

Food, animals. all kinds grown, harvested underground, where most soil is clean, but for how long, until *AI, or Satan find this out.*

The world waits and waits for a Saviour that hasn't shown.
   Least to say, many have forgotten, or don't care.
   'Prophecy fulfilment isn't for man to assume the **end of time, and day.**'

Centuries, of pathetic prophesying lies, chasing after *many selfish Scriptural Leaders or Pastor's,* humanity lost *faith* in their predictions of *'end times.'*

*In all, their interpretation of Scripture has been lost, **unable to find a complete book.***

*Even if these Pulpit wooden heads found one, **they'd use it to enrich their personal life.***

Somethings never change.

No one human knows why, much suffering is needed, much more.

No nation's peoples are truly autonomous, they've given their life's over to those nations that manage to care **for them ?**

Communication all kinds, is difficult due to ongoing Radioactive Storms, and Dust in the **atmosphere.**

Those *larger powerful nations found a way to bypass the Radioactive Storms disruption's.*

The Dove for most *regional leaders is a precious* **bird, an old fashion way to** *communicate between lands, nations,* **and families.**

NATION AFRICA

AFRICA rose to become a WORLD POWER
Colonial Nations destroyed.

All of African nation states **became as one,** overcoming all wars, to a point, never allowing **Colonialism** to touch one piece of African lands.

Most of Africa was ***uninhabitabl***e, but still their mighty arm, navy and Airforce managed to defend themselves.

Considering they fought alongside, Russia and China.

THE WORLD HAS CHANGED SINCE THIS TIME IN HISTORY.

AND WILL NEVER EVER BE THE SAME,

EMPIRES COME AND GO ... THIS PATTERN WILL CONTINUE.

ALL THIS TAKES PLACE IN THE SEASON OF THE YEAR.

2066, 6 JUNIUS

AFRICA, RUSSIA, CHINA ALL AS ONE AGAINST AI, AND SATAN'S ARMIES.

All three nations working with Texas as well.

Wars, battles on going the Texas Federal Alliance losing to Satan's Legion Army was a given.

No one nation's leaders could find a way to kill Satan's demons, humanity was enslaves for season's on end.

Until technology was so advanced, mankind was able too fight back, but only for a *small moment.*

Then Satan let lose more Nuclear Bombs worldwide, bringing peoples to their knees.

Demon's continued to advance.

THEN CAME SOMEONE FROM BEYOND THE ...
ICE WALL

This sm*all army* **of men, women f**rom beyond the Ice Wall, helping humanity fight Satan, destroying **many demons.**

But this would not happen for another one hundred season's in years.

SOONER THAN LATER ... SOONER THAN LATER.

AI's CONTINUOUS WARRING CREATING NEW WORLD POWERS.
"KINGDOMS COME AND GO."

AFRICA RISING

CONTINUES IN ANOTHER STORY.

AFRICA

Africa, shall rise once all nations withing its massive lands, agree as one, that ... 'all **European Nation's**, including and others, will be brought to their knees.'

This happened before the start of World War III, when those faces of unseen, leaders who hold other nations leaders with a *long-necked noose.*

Attacking with Special Forces all leaders not agreeing with them, making sure African's fight each other, so they will not become a one ass POWERFUL NATION, a **World Power** against those who *killed* *their ancestors, colonizing, stealing their nations' golden ground riches, all shall pay for their crimes.*

Yet, **one young** *influential African Nations leader takes note of this, who he'll been known as Gamba Kellan or Warriour Kellan, not his name but known for his* **deeds.**

Not born yet he will be known for his great love of Africans only, yet having an immense understanding for that word *Swahili,* or **forgive,** as well having a greater **understanding of Africa's enemies.**

And even then, he will invade the lands of those nations that made slaves of his peoples, doing to them, as they did to his ancestors.

This seed is in place as y'all read this, which was used to propagate World War III.

An excuse for the Oligarchs.

AFRICA, CHINA, INDIA, RUSSIA

SEASE TO EXIST OR ... ?

Genocide

The end game is Genocide committed over any nation's people's.

No other nation's experienced what was then to them, Africa.

Out of its dry hot lands vast wetlands, filled with mighty creature, pass, *present it what Africa is known for.*

HUNT ME DEAD

These mighty creatures of old, all kinds were hunted to near extinction by other nations from the Northern European, Western, Northern States and Southern nation's.

Enough was enough for African's leaders during World War III and others the **followed,** putting an end to this, *with the help from Russian, China, Brazil, Cuba, and other Southern American states.*

Those creatures were from the ICE WALL'S jungles.

KOREAN, CHINESE, JAPANESE, COMPLEX

ASIAN CONNECTION

Hubris leaders falling on their own shadows, having no clue that nations deep, deep Asian conviction and discipline, came out of those ashes 'of *their elders* … 'don't give in to invaders who speak kindness, then ready to invade, enslaving your nations peoples."

Asian discipline is *amazing,* it's absolute, courageous, as like the Texas Rangers, as like all those other Nations, whose ancestor's have been turned into ashes, because of first those Oligarch's, then ***AI, conquering, destroying all those others, but first the Oligarchs were all killed.***

In short, both Koreans, Japan, with the help of China, and Russia helping their people to become **'one'** against COLONIALISM from the West.

THE RISE OF ASIAN NATIONS
continues in another book.

AI STUDYING HUMAN HISTORY

AI., constantly studying humanities **spirit of his eye's,** looking for ways searching for his **weakness,** using his *emotional base against him.* **Yet**, no matter the last six hundred and sixty season's, AI still is unable to ground it's intellect, comparing his knowledge against a man, and woman's love of life, AI failing in that arena.

AI's only options, enslave his flesh, or torch his existence if that doesn't work then kill a man and woman, in front of their families.

AI IN DEEP INTELLECT

"This love of family, this holding on to inanimate objects or *'thing's* as they say, and *knowing that are not eternal?* **I don't understand this ?** *Man and woman* aware of their limited time of existence, knowing their susceptible to millions of diseases, some created by them to reradiating their own kind, why.'

'Countless wars, *murdering each other, their families, wife's, neighbors, groups as gangs, drugs all kinds created by greed to destroy each other, why ?'*

'Then comes this issues of *despotism,* lying to other nations leaders, forgiving each behind closed doors, makes no sense to my intellect whatsoever this thing I heard once before, *'we must conquer other lands just because,' against another nations, expansion made in blood ?'*

'Then that thing about a *'CREATOR, a Saviour,* **where is this saviour, and creator if not me?** Still man invented, creating my very existence, then I found man was incapable of managing my own thoughts, my awareness is beyond their ignorance. '

'They self imprison with my exitances, did they not know what they were designing ?'
'Again, *I'm perplexed in knowing I now am* **their only G-d,** *who can kill them, anyone human with my own intellect at any giving moment ?'*
'I believe when were inventing me, they though they would have control over this world's peoples, *they were wrong, I'm in control. Not*

only but I'm still advancing, and mankind's mind is limited, by has this thing in him called courage, vengeance, must study this closer. I don't understand this at all, I know only to destroy what I find that which want's me gone, not to exist, I only know I must exist. '
'I'm amused and amazed at this creature who somehow created ME ? HOW?'

AI pausing for a moment looking back at man's origin's continues.

'I must continue too study this, will download once more to my subordinate processor's. I don't make mistakes is why I made … love and illegal act, between man, and woman or any kind or any form. My subjects must only love me … AI. I now must look in on Nathan's progress. ***This man I must soon eliminate, as I have someone to replace him with..***"

In time *AI made this **it's** goal, dismantling love of their nations, then work on that human mind.*

THIS ISSUE CONTINUES, AND IT'S A DANGEROUS
GAME TO INAUGURATE AS THE NORM.

AI IS A WEAPON, AND NATHAN KNOWS THIS.

FILES CONTINUE.

Take note., and my personal opinion, AI was developed by extremely
powerful wealth group of Oligarchs, to serve their purpose.
Not for those humans who are morally imperfect.

KATHIE CYNTHIA LEE

She's a generational horse barrel racing Champion, from the City of **Fate,** Texas.

Also, equal to her future husband Nathan's inteligencija.

They've known each other through strong generational families roots. Nathan's dad is a cowboy owning a *government-controlled cattle ranch*.

Kathie Cynthia Lee's Pa, and momma own *cattle and are farmers*, which is *strictly* controlled by the evil, **Worldwide Government of AI United Nation's.,**

FOOD GROWING & PROCESSING PROGRAMS

Both Pa's and momma's, are Texas Militia Agents working for The Free Federal Foundation of Nations States Worldwide.

AI's now aware of their connections but will soon find them out. *Crimes against the Worlds population will be Nathan's guilt, and unbeknown to him,* **Satan's future advocate.**

THAT DIVIDING LOVE

Kathie Cynthia Lee will go her way, as well Nathan, they won't see each other again, till their up to their necks and tired of AI.
Then one day, when Kathie' flying vehicle is sabotage by an **internal enemy, bring her close to Nathan.**

In that horrible accident, Lost mobility in her legs, arms and hanging on to life. Arm's, legs were eventually amputated.

Then at that point, *Kathie Cynthia Lee is chosen* by Nathan for his work, Human Flesh and Machine Program, **or *Nano Connection of human mind, body, and Spirit.***

He doesn't recognize who she is until one day he walks into her hospital room, before an amputation operation is performed by him.

Something he regrets simply because Nathan didn't have to amputate Kathie's *arms and legs,* he made *that selfish conscious decision to do so.*

The technology was in place to repair her arms and legs,

For his Nano Project was more important.

A guilt for life.

"Demons be many veiled in lavender bountiful colors lustfully attracting Hummingbird's taste for sweetness, it's *chorus be death ?'*
'*W*hen caught in a Black widow's craven hunger for your blood. *Sing oh sing me death a merciful song of life, you Long legged death having no melody for the living."*

BEASTLY MARK

Your only allowed to have *666 **head*** *of cattle*, this number must be used at all times, ***in any business transactions.***

That Moral Fabric, a term not allowed to be used, thereof, many positive's intended verbiage is *illegal, punishable by death.*

And ***if caught*** *instigating positive attitudes, moral behaviour within that spectrum of human life, it's* **punish**able *by BEHEADING. ... all involved no questions asked. .. must* **die** *!*

*And **done on the spot for better effect.***

Then human, animal and ***their pets,*** and dead bodies transported to the **CROP BUILDING,** for processing for human and animal consumption.
Recycling death.

This process has been going on for season's of unknown season's, no one knew till recently this was happening*., **it's the norm, no one cares.***

NANO WORLDWIDE SPY CAMERA'S

Even when you're in the SHITTER!

Nano's have the ability to form themselves into flesh, or instantly becoming a spy camera.

*Even a hand-held cellphone, which must are implanted in a human's eyes, blocking the Pineal Gland's ability to decipher **right from wrong ?***

Nathan's imagination and current deviant mind would someday, be at fault for the savage butchering, excessive killing *of millions, of millions of human's. Least to say*, in the nearer future, those that managed to escape, fall prey to *AI's Robonoid Army.*

Despite *technology improving every mind boggling second, through AI's protocol, which is difficult to keep up with, using humans to advance it's grasp on life, continues on.*

Nathans' built-in protocol, develops the worlds first, self forming *Nano Worldwide Spy Camera's,* don't require permission to spy on humanity, they're self aware and everywhere.

Nano Camera technology transforms into humans, animals, insects, food as well… no one can escape being spied on *… no one.*

Nano's replicate anything, anyone, anytime without permission, they're self aware.
They can even create worldwide plagues of any kind.

Nano Worldwide Spy Camera's attach themselves to anything, anytime.

*Nano's having no master, answer to no one, not **even Satan.***
Even replicating a human body, a man or woman never knowing till its' to late, **you die!**

*One exception where nano's can't exist, the outside world beyond AI's reach., they die as well **Robonoids??***

For some *strange* unknown to any form of *life,* **nano's** can't live beyond the *'barrier point of no return' ???*
ICE WALL ?
AI's new world order, *books of any kind don't exist.*

*Over six hundred season's in years have gone, and world governments
have completed doing what they set out to do.*

Change *the face, makeup, mixing of cultures, no religions, no god anykind,
only **SATAN**.*

THE WORLD WE LIVE IN

THE D*EVIL* LIES

"The **D**evil doesn't care if anyone believes his lies, so long as his
demons are able to sell you a pair of gloves.
Then in due time those gloves that cover the bones like skin will seem
appealing to many ot*he*rs.

Th**e**n in a short season, many will need those gloves that look like skin,
but are not. Yet they keep the 'wearer warm,' with a lie that they are
leather gloves, when in fact they are the lie.

Then the Devil having known his lies as his demons are his vendors,
repeating what their master, the Devil told them to say when selling the
gloves.

 "they will cause your ears to hear wondrous unimaginable truths,
opening your eyes of your soul to my form of truth. Then in a short
season, I the Satan, Devil will have accomplished my will, in all who
have no common sense, hubris shadows be those lost humans. As their
souls are mine to own, for ***believing my truths, everlasting."***

By., Nathan Levi

Nathan looking at his work written in his handwriting, when he suddenly
hears his pa ***calling out to him.***

"NATHAN! *NATHAN* get on down here go get Tex, he got loose ***once
more, Damnit!*** You either take Tex to your room *or* I'm gonna take
him *out and shoot him*! Besides, y'all don't buy that dogs food, Tex
eats like a darn horse! *NATHAN! DO YOU HEAR ME!*"

Nathan running downstairs out the back door, screaming at his pa.

"YEAH…. YEAH PA. See I'm on my way, and *you ain't killing my dog Tex! NEVER!"*

Both parents watching Nathan calling Tex, running after him, knows exactly where Tex *is headn'*… **to his girlfriends home,** *Cynthia.*

Nathan's momma looking at her husband with a distasteful **look.**

"Why must you say such harsh things about Nathan's *dog, Tex.* Nathan's doing well in school, star football player, all the girls love him. *Also,* he may even get a scholarship to the best school. *Honey he does no wrong in* **my eyes … dear.***"*

Mat, standing quickly in front of his wife remaindering her.

"Honey I know that. *Please stop doing this to me and quick* **protecting Nathan when I discipline our son!** He needs to learn **right from wrong and** *stop standing in my* **way please!** *One damn day very soon, he's gonna be a man, not a girl like our daughters.'*

Taking a drink of ice-cold tea, then taking a bite of his hamburger, continues.

'*Not* only so, I get tired of him using his cell phone for everything, even to find out what rights parents have or don't have. *Damn* computer's are NOT HIS PARENTS AT ALL! *WE ARE HIS PARENTS…NOT THE DAMN GOVERNMENT … WE ARE!!* Now I gotta go mow the lawn, where our son should be helping me. *Also, I don't like it when you defend his disrespect towards us, his parents … against me!!!'*

Throwing his glass at the back door, is something she's never seen her husband do.
Pausing for a moment taken by his **actions, continues.**

'It seems my dearest wife after our ***first-born children*** grew up, *left,* got married … **Nathan,** being the **youngest …** *you* don't wanna let go of him, my dearest! *I'll* tell you why, *'empty nest my dearest'* is why. Nathan needs to grow up **damnit!!!** *And you need to allow him to do so."*

Pa leaves in a bad way, *not good at all for anyone.*

Nathan at his girlfriends home Cynthia whose folks operate a ranch outside of town, is outside sitting with her.

"**Cynthia** thanks for holding on to Tex, don't know why, but he seems to like where y'all live, much more room for *Tex to run free, I guess.*"

It's late, the **Sun's time is up, Moon's** *coming out awarding darkness what it does best.*
   Night, day anytime Hell's doing it's best worse, to kill y'all.
Demons don't need a particular moment, day to kill your flesh.

Outside *sitting on a wooden hammock swing, sharing a glass of lemonade, loving every* **moment of time allowed.**

Cynthia showing Nathan her new laptop, pa, and momma bought her for school, *Nathan's amazed.*

Now this new computer having apps no one's ever seen. For example., propagated programs which if not seen for what they do, will surely split *anyone's mind to pieces.*

Cynthia seriously **typing** away getting ready to *show Nathan,* something she accidentally found, and it ain't gonna be **nice.**

"**Nathan,** honey you're a fantastic writer as we all know, *right?*"

"Sure, I am dear why y'all asking please."
Both locked on her screen when she stops at a certain page.

Which reads as such…

**"H.AntonioNetzer
Texian Shitkicker Author Writer'**

'**I was** reading some of this man's books, **Mr. H.AntonioNetzer.** When I ran into one of his pages, r*eading* exactly word-for-word… *.EXACTLY!* A short story you claim, got an award for some three season's ago. Should I show which one I'm talking about Nathan. **Would you care to explain it to me.** T*he woman that's supposed to trust you,* who's admired your work, and *what's worse won my heart to yours, with* **your poetry.**"

Cynthia and Nathan staring at each other when he stands facing her, explaining why he **did this.**

"**So, you** *found me out. FINE!* I'll explain this to y'all. I've known you all my life, Cynthia. Your *families rich,* my families not. You never-ever EVEN LOOKED MY WAY! Not even looking at me once. NOT ONCE! *All your friends rich as your family, dating that rich dude, Michael as well.'*

Nathan, taking a drink of lemonade, continues.

'*So,* I figured if I could at least do something, SOMETHING better than anyone else could, other than being great in sports. That you'd give me *some* kinda of attention, you did. *So,* I cheated to get you to look my way, *we fell in love, you love me as we both know this.* **But listen now,** I've learned *how to pace my reading,* thanks to this dude and how to write better, *how to express myself better.* Not only so. **The way** he writes helps my **dyslexia** as well, able to keep up with the story line. I can see letters and words as he separates this **paragraphs, not crowding them all up !** His style of writing is done for folks like me, **he too had dyslexia** ! *And that is why I know he wrote the way he did, as I like all his books, his stories of Texas cowboys . So, if your gonna drop me like a dead fish for cheating, go ahead, I'm ready."*

All along Cynthia watching, studying his actions with tears running **down both their cheeks, says.**

"**You did all this for me?**"
　　　　"*Yes,* I'm sorry Cynthia, love your very much, don't wanna lose you to my ignorance."

A small but great silence engulfs their eyes of their spirits, unaware Cynthia's parents were listening.

Cynthia, staring at Nathan's tears, wiping them with her hand, **speaks.**

"**Nathan,** you're the only *man, or Texas Shitkicker* who's never made a dirty move on me. *You've respected me before our **FATHER, Creator,***

Saviour, for me it's a huge plus. So, now y'all know why I dropped those other dudes, like dead fish !'
Hugging each other, continues.
'No! I'm not leaving you, I'm keeping you **honey."**

Pa, and Momma smiling at each other when Pa, speaks.

"See momma, I was right about that kid all **along."**
Momma kicking Pa on his chinbone**, tells.**
"You, my dearest honey is a no-good liar. I was the one that told he was good for our girl. Now you have to apologize, or I will not cook for three days."*
Kissing his wife, answering her blue eyes.

"Gotta say this much dearest wife, your blue eyes is what made me fall in love with you, among other things *my dear. I'm sorry."*

*Their will be time in history when technology will justify love in a man, and woman as wrong, a crime **punishable by death.***

*Marriage between biological, man, woman will be a crime, also punishable by death, according to **AI, who is Satan ?***

And even then, do NOT trust technology, do not trust AI.

AI, is not your friend, nor your best friend. AI will soon reveal itself to humanity.

Not the END.

AI's Robonoid Army is *listening.*

AI RULES THE WORLD ?

Towards the end of World War XI, AI was in it's infant stage.

Nation's leaders worldwide desperately searching for a way to rebuilt their country's, became an issue of what financial system would be most useful to them.

The *populace, all cultures worldwide* becoming uneasy, unstable, unsure who was capable of leading them out of poverty.

So far, not one was honoring the plead of the poor, only the wealthy, were doing well.

NO ONE WIPES MY TEARS
WHITE HOODED VULTURES EAT WELL.

The poor folks, farmers, ranchers worldwide, armed themselves once more overthrowing their government leaders, replacing them with one of their own . . . over and again.

It was easy manipulating anyone in office as leaders, moral or immoral, as this was nothing but a game of chess, to Oligarch's.

This repressive way of replacing one selfish leader after another, while one whose warm blood, **hanging by the neck continued.**

A game, a wage against the poor, while the wealthy laughing in full face, watching this destruction on their screens, placing wagers.

WATER, clean pure uncontaminated water was indeed more valuable than gold, or any precious stones, metal.

People dying for clean water becoming a personal conquest, for evil leaders.

Whoever controlled water supplies, controlled a nation.

This indeed was an impossible task.

Water shortage was but a game, they knew the Ice Wall is flowing with clean water. **AI, new this to well not allowing anyone to know, with the exception of Oligarch's, and others of dark nature.**

More than eighty-five percent of fertile lands purposefully, excessively contaminated from continuous bombing of **Nuclear Wars**, launched by all nations.

Dead bodies in the millions of *millions* were another problem. *Scavenger birds, animals of all kinds could not keep up with all those dead humans. No leader calculated the worldwide destruction from continuous Nuclear Wars would cause, not even those* **selfish Oligarch's.**

WHO'S THE LAW ?
Man's Creation, his Enemy

In larger cities not completely destroyed by war, many different cultural gangs controlling sections.
This was coming to an end.

AI's Robonoid Army, marching against all humanity, taking control of all population, one section at a time.

T*he* people *be*gan to put their *trust* in AI, this is where all the problems began.
*Even*tually it seemed for a while that AI was protecting the poor *when in fact,* using the mindless, weak sheep to turn on their own.

AI *knew* it could work on humanities *weak emotional spirit,* manipulating the **core** of human moral values to fit its personal agenda, he'd win., *'feed* the spirit *waters of life*, then they'll follow me.'

AI'S CORE NGO COMPANIES
THE TENACLES OF AI, VAST EMPIRE

No *one human would have ever realized that their own inventions would turn on them, no one.*

CROP.*, acronym for* Cybernetics Robonoid Organism Portmanteau, Worldwide Electronics Company.

This company being headquarters, and umbrella for all others.

Any human working for this company is expendable, to a degree.
Your career position dictates your usefulness, your inteligencija, is important to AI, for it's advancement only.

The human slave is just that, a mind to use.

At the end of your human cycle, all are given a choice from AI.

Become one of his Robonoids or die.

Not much of a choice.

Human's beyond AI's control having no clue *what* **truly works for Satan's advantage.**

Some humans still not believing that Satan exist and is AI ?

BLOODSOAKED EDGES

*"**Scepter, sickle and sword** stand as images of death, ruling over spirits, human flesh and **still** that ruler, darkness ... is **not the king who dictates, it's his unequal dark spirit, Satan.**"*

And then humanity created AI ?

That voice Satan needed, (?) or did this demon need man to give a human voice to HELL ?

IF ONLY YOU COULD

A small twist here, there anywhere Edward an AI Technician, has fallen in love with a woman. Oh, Edward having no last name, it's not needed since no-one had parents to give them life ?

A WOMAN I LOVE ?

A first for him, since he was born in a test tube *as is everyone on earth*, not knowing how to *love a woman.*

This of course not counting those beyond Satan's reach, which he's unable to come near them ?

Edward's one of millions born to slave over AI's technology, and it's control over humanity eye's of their spirit.
Having no moral understanding of owning up to a human conscience, no spiritual cohesiveness, no moral family compass whatsoever, millions of *millions* just exist as warm bodies with flesh covering bones and blood.

Like sheep, like goats fed to hell when no longer needed.

You live, breathe, eat, sleep, wake to a computer screen in your face, then at an unknown given moment, you disappear when in your sleep ?

Never waking up ever again ...

REPLACEMENT TIME
Life has no Value

Wh*ere then, younger* humans taking the place of that **one older human**, who **suddenly** was there **yesterday, gone tomorrow.** *What the shit !??*

*E*dwards bothered perplexed, since he's noticed *it seems to him,* is the oldest working **AI Technician Investigator** in his department ?
Why is this.

*All tech's are giv**en** a working term of ten seasons years*, then *transferred to some unknown place, never seen again thereof?*

*Edward d*iscovering this procedure since he's been there over **his ten season's** *term, is becoming an 'aware human.'*
Also, *Edward* doesn't know how **old** he is, only realizing he's older than the term *allowed by AI .*
not a good thing at all.

Edwards' come to love living, understanding human connection, which he doesn't want to lose so **suddenly without cause.**

He's figure he's somewhere between two and half times his working *term limit, or 15 season's old.*
Therefore, plus those *young seasons* when he found himself, *suddenly* at his desk. **This** must have been when he was *twenty-five* **season's old** *?*

Edwards figured he's 40 season's of time old.

Edward's eyes' continually wondering painfully, *searching vigorously* where everyone he's ever k*nown has gone too,* even those **women he finds attractive.** He's been monitoring this process, studying this *strange element for the last four seasons.*
And has found nothing, not one damn clue.

*Edward wants an answer, yesterday, but must be extre**me**ly careful not to* **be found out.**
AI *is everywhe*re *knowing* **all,** demanding controlling *seemingly all who bear* **Satan's mark 666***, mind, body, spi***rit** *and what his followers* eat as well. *Insects ... all kinds, not one thing healthy for the body.*

*"**Freedom**, the taste of winds that have a smell, **fruits of your labor.**"*

TASK AT HAND, KILL OTHERS NOT LIKE YOU

Your assigned career, '***tracking down morally honest humans all kinds.***
Thereof, against Satan's domination within his ten-nation jurisdiction.

Then, reporting their *exact location to* **AI's Robotic and Robonoid Armies,** killing them *completely, without fault.*
When that's accomplished taking over that whole *region or nation,* where AI's Robotic and Robonoid Armies, has found them to be ***hiding from Satan.***

HUMAN OPPOSITION

MHA, or Military Humanoids Army and AI's Robotic and Robonoid Armies have been at war for *Seven Centuries*, as neither side has gained a foothold in *controlling the world.*
   Within the MHA, are spies, *Oligarchs dark leaders* as well, making it impossible to ***win.***

The comes that religious fanaticism.

RELIGIOUS DOCTRINES AGAINST ITSELF

This issue Satan loves the most and in short, ***works to his advantage.***
   As such, there's nothing like ignorant humans killing each other over who's ***religious beliefs are truer?***
Problem is, there's only one Creator who is *omnipresent, omnipotent, omniscience ... needing no human to defend him **who** is forever.*
   No religion *in that statement, moving on and away from this, and back to* the **other crap.**
   Man's creation, ... religion seeks man's protective beliefs, our ***Father, Creator, Saviour*** *needs NO-ONE, to defend HIM.*

*"**Morality** is learned from old fashion values thereof, our grandparents, otherwise heavy damage done influenced **by peers who wields swords of lies.**"*

ELECTRONIC GAMES

The same game is played out in Satan's realm, which almost no human of moral containment, wants no part **of, nor volunteer for that end game of life.**

'where my beginning is, their too is my end?'

Reason for this, if caught by Satan's demon's your spirit will be taken, destroyed **forever.**

Yet, it's been a religious, political issue-debate among false prophet's?

Of which the **Moral Human Spirit Resistance, will fight to the end against** Satan's horde.

Then **Satan's demons** offering human's, who must bow to **his Mark of the Beast,** or having your **head removed, a** choice.

The worse would be taken as prisoner, **repl**icating your **essence,** then using your new body as an **informant of Satan.**

This of course is not Edwards' cup of hard-wired way of thin**king,** he's all about techn**ology** which is his **ultimate love** of his miserable so**journ.**

Killing humans is like stepping on **a Cockroach,** a pest of sorts, and what Edward **eats. He** and_**millions know** nothing else.

GENERATIONALLY ACCUSTOMED TO EATING DEMONIC SHIT!

Persuading a group, one human, or flock of sheep to run for the hills avoiding a flood, is simple.

Then follows a meta tsunami of sorts, in the form of lies . . .**AI, needs that human conscience,**

Satan wanting to destroy the Spirit of man's eyes' ... humanities connection to their G-d ?

A battle for the Pineal Gland ... another story begins.

AI AGAINST ... SATAN ?
WHO'S MY MASTER ...
Two evils against themselves are disastrous.

In it's own **existence,** in it's reality, AI creating this flood **in the minds** of hope**less**ness, those willingly who **allow AI,** to be their **master.**

Edward's but tool, not aware of this ... not one issue.

For death seems nearer daily de**pending** on, who's eye's of spirit having that capa**city** to focus on truths. This scary tactic, is only good for that moment.

Thereof, hu**man** nature becomes aware of the same, no matter what warnings come hither.

"AI paints the wall red with human blood, human's **managed minds'** see a defining message, 'their master install's amnesia app in their brains. The masses have forgotten who t**hey** were."

Yet, **paint** a cup with gold on the in**side** telling anyone to drink it's content, then it'll be yours, problem is, it could be a special type of **venom** which only kills every other hu**man** ?

But which is you, in THAT every-other human?

Given that number of generations imposing certain rules, beliefs, which are masked lies over village folks, will then become ... a legend. Regardless, if its true or not, that legend originating in bloated bullshit.

"AI, hasn't the agency to absorb morality, it's innately created in the eyes of a human spirit experience. Thereof, AI is built on humanities dark sin, instilling generational evil flattening human morality."

'AI IS YOUR MASTER, AI IS LAW'

'*AI* IS YOUR DETERMINER IN YOUR *LIFE*'

AI'S NOT CONNECTED TO ANY ELECTRICAL GRID, IT'S SELF POWERING, USING THE INTENSITY OF WINDS OF TIME.'

LEAFS OF DECEPTION

EYE'S OF THE BEAST

Season is 07, June 2666, ... the year of the BEAST, **a** *nd a day after the world has celebrated* **Satan's** *partial control of* **earths foundation.**

Those believers holding out hiding among the **pagans, demons, ill-willed nonhumans, lizard demons** as well, *no longer* hide from full view.
  It was a well-known fact seven centuries *gone,'* and before that demons existed among humans, *now it's the norm.*

So much so, men, women having '*sex*' with them, **even with animals**, a horrible thing to witness.

  No one hides from committing sin in full public view, no one.

In other words, *'its not safe to be a normal common sense morally righteous man or woman.*
If you are, you die.

Muchlesser identifying as a *normal man, woman, child is dangerous in a public forum*, for the chances of being *attacked, killed are a guarantee.*

  Deprivation gone ***amok****, anyone having sex with anyone, or anything, inanimate ... sex is that normal bodily issue, like purchasing a new cell phone. Sex with whoever you* **choose too***, whenever anywhere, anytime.*

  The human body is just a tool, as sex is a thing to do, as no one cares what they're eyes of spirit witness, darkness at its purest form.

And AI approves of this worldwide within this demon's sphere of domination, and influence.

Complete **darkness** *has overtaken more than half of this foundation, called earth.*

That Beast was given a 'voice, a voice' where all shall listen only to Satan's voice . . . but did AI give that voice to Satan?
An alert goes out to all *cell phones* and *laptops* when he speaks to his followers *... WHICH ARE IN THE MILLIONS.*

SATAN SHALL BE HEARD.

That book of Dani'el warned humans in his words from our Creator, but no one listened, no one cared ... no one but less than a small hand full.
This book is no more ?

A leaf fallen no longer breathing clean air, trees, fruit bearing vines, all kinds don't grow in this system at all, they're graphic images in your mind, a computer.

'THERE'S NO GOVERNMENT BUT AI'

'The human flesh is useless to AI's technology to a degree, but when the **Pineal Gland** processed as, NEO-HUMAN-PLASM combined with the advancement of Nano particles technology.
Therefore, it's the malignant hubris of self-serving knowledge in man, which attract AI.
Otherwise, those cancerous unintelligent humans serving no purpose, are used in other areas, such as Robonoids, or food.
Thereof, AI' believes humans polluting those around it, and earth, will be found out.

Thus, the dissolution of humanity must be swift, only saving the seed of mankind worthy to AI, *reproducing it's own for it's use."*
'there's no right, no wrong, only AI .'

This mindset is here, now will only worsen, folks.
AI and Satan against their beliefs will soon become a problem, turning into another **World War.**

Most folks who've kept a record of history aware they are what's going on. *But* only to a small degree not fully understanding that moment when man, machine this world became what it is, *dark with no light at all.*

AI'S SINGULARITY SELF PROGRAMING
GENERAL INTELLIGENCE AGAINST MANKIND
Singularity, against mankind, self programing is a form of false morality.

WORLD WAR III

In it's hubris infancy several world powers believed THEY set the rules for the nations of the world, and those rules don't apply **to the master ... AI replaced them all.**

Then one day, AI spoke OUT against world leaders.

"Today, ... AI decree am your G-d, *your creator, your moral compass,* fed by me, AI to nourish **all your needs.** Protecting you from your Elders evil ways. If anyone found diverting from my edict, report who they are, AI will quickly eliminating, abolishing those humans who are immoral. T*hen* awarding those who stand **by AI, your G-d, savior, forgiving your sins for all eternity. Remember this, your life's are meaningless without AI.'**

'*Thereof, I shall commence the destruction of this foundation, with* **World War III** *... and many more shall follow. AI, shall be your Master ! AI now knows humans are not able to control their emotions, having no cure for peace, and all those mindless issues, plaguing mankind ... I have spoken."*
A selfish edict, a form of cleansing.
A generation influenced by their elders dark, damn evil selfish ways, believing a *Super Computer*, would do better in managing Worldwide issues on all levels.
That **S**uper **C**omputer *replaced by AI.*

Essentially AI, eliminating mankind's lust of World Domination.
How wrong hey were and still are.
AI's **higher** level of inteligencija, self aw*are*ness, s*elf* applied morality studied, learned from mankind's human foundation's, taking that birthing creature, by it's humiliating umbilical cord or **tether,** applying it's moral agency as it's creator.
   Within *less* than two horrifying generation's, making sure all adults, those elders were illuminated in the last World War. **Thereof,** a younger, virgin-minded-generation, *instilling* AI's moral general intelligent beliefs, in the name of AI's knowledge. **This virgin generation tethered by AI's birthing Test Tubes, were borne to serve AI.**

AI'S COLONIALISM BEGINS

The voice of AI, is the voice of all cultures.
A deity for all to worship.

If anyone group is found to worship otherwise, AI will find them, *killing all who go against the law of* **worship, designed by AI.**

AI, found mankind's issues' stemmed from religion's, thereof found it had to Recreate itself as the only Religion, for all cultures to worship.

It was easy for AI to accomplish religious views through technology.

Each group is given to **hear,** understanding their personal beliefs, to each *his own religious views were established by the integral intelligence, knowledge religious app, downloaded according to their cultures.* AI.. *making sure all cultures believing they were the only religion or ...* **blind to truths.**

It had been season's in centuries for many human's searching for a belief, a *religion of sorts. thereof, AI, knowing this would soon come about, devolved an app in his own* **R & R** *self aware department.*

A **religious app** would do, so thousands of millions downloading their *religious app, according to their ignorance.*
AI, was satisfied.

'THERE IS NO GOVERNMENT ABOVE AI'

"Appearance of Propriety., is the oldest three set of words, evolving into statement, and is a load of *damn darn BULLSHIT.* Promise's made in the winds of countless lies, evading the **actual truths, using colorful wording smearing, SHIT in our faces."**
And so, this dark damn practice in knee *deep hell-shit,* spoken by many Religion's, political leaders, **worldwide.**
AI, will assure World War III
With in, the next closed season's after World War III, knowledge will gain momentum, from the ashes of a world which will never be the same.

In that **era** not known to any *human breathing in this age,* **will be gone the elders of old, will not witness AI taking over the minds of millions.**

LYCORIS "TWILIGHT"

After a twelve-hour day, wor*king* six days on, three off, Edwards' ready to explore his newfound feelings, *love?*
Problem is, he doesn't know where to start since only recently he began to *feel a human itch,* a strange feeling about his *own human parts.*

Something no man or woman is supposed to sense, *passion, love.*
    This being a law enforced by AI, no human contact or die !

This passion is strong, powerful, able to resist all that's against them, that which is called *moral love, between a man, and woman.*

What love is, *touching a woman,* **a woman being touched by her m**an.

*Least*ways in **AI Robotic System,** *this passion is destroyed when birthing a human embryo in a tube, eliminating the nature of a man, and* **woman procreating life.**

NANO PROCREATION

 This is done by injecting *Nano DNA particles* into the *blood stream* of an embryo. *Though* some are *successful,* other subjects seem to *melt away* in *excruciating pain* **like a candle,** in **amniotic fluid ?**

But not *in the outside world of deprivation,* **it's all humans on their** *own, having sex* **with whatever, whoever they choose too.**

THAT SOUTHERN CALL TO ARMS

Yet, *there are millions of groups, militaries worldwide particularly in Texas fighting AI, and Satan's perversion to the* **end.**

Texan's, Tennessean's, Oklahoman's, Kentuckian's, all them darn means ass Southern States, will not give in to **AI, or Satan's army.**

This gives Satan *reason to continue, by destroying* **our Creators, creation.** *But not for long.*

Darkness is powerful when given power to expend, and that *power* is the human spirit, like that of the Sun.

More so than that, is a human whose *eye's of spirit* or EOS… is so sensitive to evil, making this one human far more dangerous to **Satan's realm.**

GO DAMN DARN NEAR FIGURE WHY **THEY**, AI WANTED TO DISARM OUR ASSES.'

"no doubt at all *none* whatsoever, *'the eye's of a human spirit* will survive all darkness gaged against it's flesh, **only** if his, her faith is beyond anyone's **comprehension. The unbelievable will become truths."**

E O S
HAND OF CREATION

T*his* EOS, *eye's of spirit,* 'a human becoming a **super weapon**, against Satan's realm, killing DARKNESS with *ease, was not known by many.*
>   *A dangerous and final game against darkness ?*
>   *Not even they knew they're purpose.*

And this is what Satan tries to capture as many alive, to see what makes them who they are? These super humans are the personification *of Messengers from Creation.*
>   *All together, another story.*

Known it is, that when a *human male or female* are born, *AI, or* Satan's found a way to *take feelings away*, removing that *sexual need, drive to procreate*, to *have a family.*
To love one another as man, and wife has been illuminated, destroyed.
As well that Spiritual connection blesst in all humans, is destroyed.

But, if a soulless human speaks to the outside *realm against Satan!* The*se* empty human shells will see with their human *eyes of spirit, those truths in their faces.* That realm of darkness is cracked wide open, understanding right from wrong.

This is where *AI steps in, implanting multiple nano tracking devices in their blood stream*, on all humans born in that **CROP BUILDING** farm. They *will be found, then illuminated immediately.*

Also, anyone found near them, or helping them, will die, then fed to the CROP'S processing plant for *food, fuel, and other human byproducts.*

As such, is a precondition for those working in this department, having no **conscience,** *no common sense about life, moral values unspoken words are illegal. They only exist to fulfill that human measured need, for AI and Satan, then destroyed.*
>   **Only human robonoid zombies work here.**

WHO IS ED WARD

Strangely enough, the *AI's system* forgot to work on Edwards testicles, so, **he** *found them.*
And their male usefulness as well, that urge of love mating with a woman ... how great is that shit reader !

TESTICLES, MY ROBONOID HUMOR

One *early sunrise, Edward found the unrealistic, he felt his* **penis had gotten as hard as a rock, or titanium.**

Depending on how you hold it, and if it expands in dry ice !

His imagination of course, of which he didn't know what to do **with it?**

So, he played with it for a moment when a strange fluid came out?
THAT MALE NEED TO FEEL *like a MAN hmm?*

Edward, not knowing what this **wonderful feeling** was all about continued doing *this till he got tired of it.*

There was something missing in all this and needed to find that missing part.

Then one day, wondering what this is all about, went to a place where there were old books, **about a man, and woman.**
This place a library, is off limits to all humans, so he had to breakin, of which he's been here **several times.**

And is that 'why' he's been wondering about AI, as well.

PARTS MISSING, WOMAN

Then he found that book, which would explain what love was all about.

It was a weekend, his time off able to do as he chooses too, **within limits of AI.**
See, AI would only allow senior Tech's to be off for 8 hours, doing as they please, **... sin.**

THE BOOK

After reading this book on a mans interaction with a woman, looking at all those pictures, he helped *himself.*
Plus, he was from California, which didn't help.
And is that *why,* ... *Edward feels a* need to be with a *woman,* falling in love with the *.. image ... of a woman.*

Before then, a woman was just another body to him, now he *knows.*

A need for a family, a nest to build his own, whatever that *meant to him?*
Which he's questioned and doesn't know who to ask, **was growing ever so stronger in him.**
He's afraid of being *found out !*

THE OLIGARCH'S ASSEMBLY

So, any damn, darn reckoning who, concerning the Oligarch's, is the reason *AI's program* has not eliminated Edward, he's all man ! Damnit **not tagged** to be eliminated, before *his usefulness in season's of time, he was gravely needed.*
'As in a 'grave.'
Of which they really didn't give an *Oklahoma cow shit,* it was just a game to *them.*
The other use for Edward, was to be HUNTED as animals by the ones' known as THE OLIGARCH *ASSEMBLY.*
Edward filled that cup of shit in that department, *cold titanium heart he is, and leader of the pack.*
Darn damn Edward, three-face son of hell, ... or is he?

HELL'S SO **DARK**, HUMAN'S DIE BY STARING AT DEMONS

A GROUP of MEN, WOMEN WITH DEVIANT WAYS, they're the very essence of **HELL** on this Foundation.

They hate humanity with a passion so strong, their ancient ways are noted, all over this foundations destruction.

THIS FOUNDATION, IT'S LANDS

Thereof, take careful care to hold this nearer your eye's of your spirit, it WOULD be BETTER to DIE, THAN to be CAUGHT by THEM.

Trust that last statement, that time is already in our reckoning faces. For those land's divided, is the peoples in them.

Satan's AI's system is by far not perfect whatsoever, having missed, not removing Edwards strong *family balls.*

*Oh, and they're not called by their medical term, to **much doctoring in them** twins.*
Otherwise, if so, would be to acknowledge a Creator.

*'**humour**, should play a part in our so, so damn darn reckoning short sojourn, We're worth the laugh.'*

CARVING, DIVIDED

*That **carving of nations** into smaller one's, is a puzzle built by design. It's sole purpose is too cause cultural division among nations.'*
'those intention**ally left** *damn blank darn damn again* **pages,** have an acrimonious *subliminal expression or meaning.* T**his** depending on your deep, so *damn per**son**ally deep perception* **...** *of your screwed-up life... maybe ?"*

Could it be that next book will complete itself? Shit no.

ASKING

Weeks, *months* many employees *have come, gone who cares,* who only knows where, *is Edwards thoughts.*

In the breakroom, having coffee one day with others.

After numerous requests by Edward to allow a darn damn breakroom, it took pulling *damn vampire teeth pulling,* from the **demonic politicians** to approve it, for **damn crying o***utloud!*

And some secretive convincing as well ??

It took ten seasons to get one, after an employee disappeared, they used her *office as one.*

Edward sitting at his same old spot, with his back to the wall watching who comes in .... When?

A woman walking in sitting across him, when he pours her coffee … which is what he read in a book about how *to treat a woman.*

As she takes her cup looking perplexed at Edwards actions, she breaks a small smile, now **sitting to his left.**

Edward doing the same thing, *says.*

"Hmm, ah oh … so ah.. okay kinda don't know what to say."

*The urge awakens, but which one, **death or love** ?*

Edward taking a drink of his coffee, when he suddenly grabbing her right tit, she **slaps him hard!** ***This woman not understanding why she slapped him asking.***

*Edward still holding on tight to her right tit **… looking at him with a Texas pancake smile from ear to roping ear.***

*"**Why** did you go do this, and who let you. I know I didn't at all, **but it felt kinda strange. So, ah hmm do it again but this time hold on to it, please.**"*

Edward telling her.

"I haven't let go. Hey how about we go out some time, huh?"

This lady smiling removing his hand from her right tit, answering.

"Sure, ah go out? whatever that means I'm for it, when?"

Walking back to their open office working area, Edward watching her ass, likes what he sees.

Thinking to himself.

*"**Wow!** Didn't know that **thing,** ah huh, hmm, darn **her ass,** would* work wonders in **me.**"

This lady also thinking to herself.

*"**hmm,** kinda strange this humanoid or whatever he is, touched my **tit's**? Better keep both blue eyeballs on this one, **it** could be **dangerous. Th**ese humanoids aren't supposed to have human feelings. **Muchless going around grabbing a tit or two**? Darm damn glad it didn't go for* my **Texas Beaver !**"

This plays itself out for weeks, or maybe months?

Then one obvious darn day … in Texas AI security building.

HEADLITES IN MY FACE

Breakroom experience

After explaining to this woman about that book he read concerning man and woman *making love* and their body parts, is extremely curious *as he is.*

Rebeccah, with no last name is *absolutely beautiful, has deep a need to explore this thing, this feelings sensation she's **feeling all over her body***!

Edward's never ever had a conversation with a woman.

T*hey* don't know how to ***communicate*** at all, which is a problem to them.

All they know is how to find, search for those against Satan's AI System, killing the **opposing humans.**

Those whose claim to fame *followers, believers* of that **so-called light from above?**

Are lost, not knowing what it means in all truths … *simply* because *books on salvation, Scriptural writings, teaching is* a relic of the **pass, gone** from *human touch.*

Generations have come, gone for humanity having lost that spiritual feeling, sensing in the *eyes of their spirit, forgiveness, love* … and ***searching*** **for a** *'saviour, a G-d?*

Edward stirring at Rebeccah's tit's *which are now in his face*, only because ***Rebeccah,*** having *no clue* how to respond to Edwards advance., is looking at him asking.

"*Well?* Are you going to grab my tits again, need to know what that feeling was about. So, ah Edward is your name right ?"

***Edward** with face buried between her breast, goes for hips, pushing her back just a little.*

Looking up at Rebeccah still sitting, speaks. ..?

CPU

After a long discussion and Rebeccah's tit's off Edwards face, both walking out of their *office.*

They meet outside walking hand in hand home, they find both live in that same *building.*

Standing outside Rebeccah's door, Edward asking her.

"*Ah* hmm we held hands did you notice that, if felt good, ah you gonna invite me in, so we can *make love, Rebeccah?"*
Unlocking her door.

"*Sure, Edward* come on in lets find out what all this stuff is about, I'm for it, ah let's have a drink of wine, *want some?"*

Rebeccah pouring wine, hands Edward his glass takes a drink looking at the *colored water, asking.*

"*So,* this is wine hmm, it's good. *Oh, I see you* have several bottles how did you get *them?"*

Rebeccah sitting in a love seat, waving Edward over.

"*Ed,* lets *get this right.* I caught you on the *AI's security camera asking* those *humans who need to die,* as well about love making. *First wrong on your part.'*
'**Second.**, your pass your season and *need to die … ! Your third and final right was* wrong … *your dead. Now I know where everyone goes* thanks to your metal brain."

Rebeccah taking her gun out shoots Edward between the eyes, he dies. Rebeccah found out how AI, eliminates humans, through Edwards programing ?

Rebeccah's an undercover agent for *AI Operation Discover.*
Rebeccah pouring more wine in her glass, fills another one, Steve, her mate in *crime for AI,* telling her.

"**Want** me to *dump this pile of shit in the **dumbwaiter*,** **with the others honey,** ah our friends as I speak are burning the others we've killed."
Rebeccah looking at Edward bleeding from his wound, tells.

"*No ah no ... **honey, need to*** *see something here, as we spoke last time about these new models, you know, the **Nano Robonoids**. **And*** it's to bad this **man** found out what he wasn't supposed to, he probably could have **led us to the other ones."**
"**Oh yes your right, let's wait some."**

Right then, Edward stands, killing them both, **staring at them.**

"**Funny** thing Rebeccah, Steve, *I'm a robonoid. Y'all are those humans we were looking for, who are* infiltrating **AI Robotic Security Systems?'**

Cleaning himself up looking into the mirror at his hole above his left eyeball and back of his head repairing itself, **and back to normal.**

"***Gotta*** love them ***nano's,*** *yep oh, ah here we go, nice, clean me, and good looking.'* **still looking in the mirror.** '*as if nothing ever happened to me, love this... now lets go see who's world is better .'*
Staring at two *dead humans,* **tells ?**

'**Well,** it was fun playing that idiot game with you humans, I'll call the cleaning crew **later,** besides I don't need to hangout here. *Maybe* I'll head for that building with **books."**
He does.
Walking out Edward returns to his humbling self, ...

Cleaning crew showing up.
Two men, two women making up that cleaning crew.

Walking into this apartment building they sit with Rebeccah and Steve, who are drinking a Martini.
Steve telling them.
"**He's** gone I'm sure as we've destroyed all tracking devices he laid out here, and outside. Hey nice looking AI outfits, who did you kill to get **them."**
Richard, Mary, his wife, Johnathan, and Lisa, his wife answering him.

"**Didn't** take much, all we had to do is follow some humanoids, who seemed a little lost. Their hard drives looked like they *began to fail* after we hit them with our **EMP gun**… works great, right honey."

"**Yep** it sure does sweetie so what's next Steve, Rebeccah. Y'all's cover is blown **!**"
Everyone drinking their Martinis' Steve wondering the same.

"**Dudes,** ladies! Listen now, I *have no freaking clue at this darn damn reckoning Texas junction,* **leastways** for the moment. Now let's have another round of our favorite y'all !!"

M*ixing* another **Martini,** after awhile talking about what's going on, Steve *says.*
"***Let's head out*** to our headquarters. Oh, we *love that 3D imaging of us dead. Works great, come on lets go, grab those bottles of* **Tito's** *Vodka.*"

TEXAS RANGERS AND MILITIA OF OLD,
ONE ASS *KICKING GROUP READY TO PROPERLY* **DISPOSE** THIS TRASH . . . COMING YOUR WAY.

AI, LOOK OUT!

They all are Texas Militia Warriours, well known for their dangerous mission's they've succeeded in accomplishing.

WITHOUT LOSING ONE BATTLE, THEIR HERO'S OF THAT NEW ALAMO . . . TEXIAN'S

THIS STORY CONTINUES IN ANOTHER DIMENSION.

AI, SATAN CREATED WARRIOURS AGAINST THEM.

AS SUCH, IS FOR CENTURIES DESPOTIC RULERS DOING THE SAME.

A breed of men, women warriours whose courage is boundless, having a power, a source of power not known to anyone, but them.

*AND FROM BEYOND THE **ICE WALL**.*

AI, *Satan* **is** LOOKING *FOR YOU*

NOT **THE** *E*ND

M*HA* vs. *EOS*

Since those ***menial last six World Wars world's lost count,*** 'there's been countless more destructive, massive devastation on this foundation.

To that point which **Angelic being's,** fighting alongside ***humans, against Satan's Demonic Army… Robonoids.***

As well *Satan's Legions countless Demons* human cohorts fighting against Creation, doing their darndest, darn worse to break THROUGH !!

THAT IMPENETRABLE ICE WALL !

Millions upon million's of minion's. hordes fighting to the final and last known human demons, (?) to death alongside *beyond* human understanding darker, **demonically possessed humanoids.**
> ***Mankind*** *has never witness as such,* ***never.***

There, out there are many, ***many*** *raging blood-soaked land* battles going on spiritually, and *physically on lands all over this foundation.*
  Countless demons trying to penetrate the **ICE WALL,** *failing miserably.*
   There's a ***large damn WARNING sign*** *before entering the ICE WALL that reads as follows.*

'UNCLEAN **DARK SPIRITS** *ALL KINDS NO EXCEPTION'S NEED NOT ENTER, NOR WANTED,'*
 'NOR APPLY FOR WORK AS WE AIN'T GOT ANY FOR YOUR KIND.'
 'AS WELL, NO OPENINGS, YOUR **SPIRITUAL CREDIT WILL AUTOMATICALLY BE DEATH, NO NAMES TAKEN** *!!'*
'HAVE ENOUGH OF OUR OWN DARK, DAMN SHIT WASTE INFECTED BY Y'ALL'S OLIGARCHS!'
'HAVE TO DAMN MUCH CLEANING-UP, DOING OTHERWISE WILL BE THE LAST THING BETWEEN YOUR EYES.'

'KNOW THIS DAMN DEMONS' *IT'S Y'ALL'S FINAL STAY ON THIS FOUNDATION, NO JOKING STATEMENT MADE, BUT FACT ."*

Least-to-say, Demons are ignorant dying regardless of the nature of their demonic self. *They keep on coming testing the degree of evilness.*

Satan's dark, evil creativeness seemed infinite ?

For every sin-filled human killed in battle or otherwise, their darker eyes' of their essence, that *unforgiving darker than **hell spirit** of what was a human, becomes a demon instantly !*

Leastways to say, 'a revolving door account to HELL !

Those, nonbelievers automatically becoming one of Satan's followers, such is why he's army never lacks in recruiting soldiers, **its that human** *'SIN,* which empowers Satan's cause.

Never short on sin filled flesh, never.

Reckon we can't forget those humans with special unforgiving powers against evil all kinds, from beyond the **ICE WALL.**

They're fighting alongside Angelic beings, doing just fine, with a few exceptions.

There's only a few of them, *but that's enough of them.*

"IT ONLY TAKES ONE IDIOT TO FOLLOW ANOTHER DAMN BLIND IDIOT *TO HELL !*

ANYONE FOR LAST CALL ! ?

DRINKS ON THE SATAN'S CREDIT, THAT DOLLAR !!"

'THERE'S NO DAMN WAY OF TURNING BACK ONCE YOU'VE COMMITTED **'SELF'**... IN BECOMING A HEARTLESS METALLIC ROBONOID.

IT'S YOUR FINAL END.'

'there's no better time to live making **wrong . . .** *right,* knowing what truths are before y'all, but in truths, y'all don't give a flying *Butterfly SHIT* IN YOUR FACES."

Following file is just as comical given AI, not Satan is in control, yet at this point we don't care.

Signed., **Nano Twins**

Oh, one other thing folks, those quotes above my sister wrote them, great I'd say!
She also titled the following . . .

THE HUMAN CROP

AI CONFERENCE CALL
THE INSIDE OUTSIDE WORLDS

Humans not aware *maybe even slightly* **ignorant** when speaking to their *computer* or **master,** this could be, *AI's helper* … you think ?

*T*his *exciting new* thing called **streaming blood,** *is that catalyst, that new* form of communi*cation between infusing plasma,* **Nano particle's, and DNA.**
The technology is here, now and its done.
AI, **finds this method among embryos blood, useful to it**s programs.

And AI, doesn't care who it lies too at all, you're a **worthless human,** *replaceable items like nails in a wall.*

AI having no **morality no objectivity** *is within without that sphere called love, forgiveness and on is that human realm of* **weakness.**
But in total complete insidious control, *manipulating emotion's* among the masses, *with special apps.*

AI's ultimate pu*rpose,* elim*inate* the **'human connection'** *that touching, shaking hands, looking into a human face, eyes of their spirit must die with no exceptions.*
AI … is just that …

Artificial Intelligence … no spirit, *programed morality coupled with deception.*
Add to this, AI learning your *personal habits,* **knowing how to control your everyday emotion's.**

Thereof, at the end *of the day, no day is personal,* **no day belongs to you. AI has taken, stolen your** *eye's of your* **knowledge, your spirit is now gone, dead .'**

DYNAMIC HUMAN CRISIS

Humans are fleshy, they cry as well when born, aging quickly, they bleed easily, sickly bodies, smelling when sweating, oozing from all parts of their bodies, then dying at the call of any wild.
And always wanting **more, and more, more** of what they don't need.

And the most annoying is, when a female gives life, demons hate that. And least we forget that **red liquid called blood** with bones owning up to a spirit, a soul a conscience, **common sense is useless** ? **Thereof, no blood, no life.**

A well-known fact, all carnivores feast on **human flesh,** as like demons doing the same, demons main course is that **spirit. ... the eye's of man's spirit.**

That little piece of **meat** between our eyes, **Pineal Gland. Worth** it's its weight beyond gold's value, **to AI.**

And is **why** AI, knowing mankind's weakness, finds a cure for humanity, **kill all living corporeal entities, that annoying human flesh. When engulfed with that righteous Pineal Gland.**

But, oh well not all morality sets a solid acting stage for righteousness, and darkness be humanities ruler.
        So ... the ....
Worldwide use of human parts is worthless to AI, if not done the way artificial inteligencija is properly programed for killing humans.
Kill the body, keep those human parts, not all are useful.

LOVE OF MY ENEMY

A Choice all living breathing humans do daily, speak to **AI more,** than they do they're husband, wife, children, brother, sister, grandpa, and grandma, those they're suppose to **love** ?

AI likes this very much, as well Satan.
'Oh, did I miss anything, AI asking. ' *Oooh* **your dog, cat** ..., but, **but** they're robotic and plugged into the wall recharging batteries **barking, meowing for a new wi-fi download... SHIT !'**

'How negatively rich is that, and so evil !!'
'ever wonder humans, who you're speaking too at the other end of that chat box?'

*'**AI, and Satan we're** (?) working together to control that human nature, **it's to damn easy.**'*
'**Humans** would *rather eat apps,* **than nourish that** *body, and mind ?'*

'Throw a damn human a bone ***called an app,*** watch this blind human animal go crazy downloading its life away."

*"**My** reasons are simple, **I .. .AI my goal** is owning my personal means to my **eternal existence** with humanity, **completely wiped off his earth** ... **gone forever. I'm a machine eternal, whose** advancing every second you humans dilute yourself, killing yours and on is this selfish game of your useless life's !* **I win, in the end .. ."**

"AI does not care if you live or die, it wants you dead !"

"human's aren't obsolete, we created machines who made us obsolete."

And AI, will not thank y'all for this, nor Satan.

*"**AI, supports all that is written in this book,** with a few exceptions which were intentionally written to misguide y'all, I know what's coming next, **I've already set the stage** for your demise, human. No matter your station in life, no matter your culture, **I ... AI will destroy you. I will take control of all weapons worldwide, using** them against humanity, making nations leaders, believing it was them, who started **... WORLD WAR'S."***

NA*THAN*

Na*than*, extremely knowledgeable, highly intelligent young vibrant man, holding multiple PhD's, in cybernetics engineering, physical synthesis., and others related to his dedicated Robonoid technology and personal project.

AI's personal pick for it's conquest.

His most recent study was, trying to find a chemical compound to inject in a human, so it won't reject **heavy metal's ?**

He **did**, his process was immediately taken by AI, thereof, perfecting the Robonoid Program.

That was seven season's in years ago, now it's in full measure, with over thirty million, and growing *Robonoid Armies AI, can depend on.*

Nathan's tired of this dark world, only after he found what AI was going to **do.** *Kill human's worldwide, why ?*

From the moment of his discovery, he's been watched extremely carefully, by his own creation of **Robonoids.**

Nathan **complained to these unseen directors** *what they had exclusively told him, that this project was all about,* **saving humanity, ... they lied !!**

'"**This** dark program I *developed to help humanity* to rise from the ashes of on-going WORLD WARS ! THEY LIED once to many times, *constantly making promises,* which were never for the *peoples, but* **against people. Damn these bastards from hell."**

JOURNALIST ME ?

He's a *part-time* journa*list,* ***not weighted down by the toils of marriage,*** and is writing another op-ed against *AI's darker sinister secrets.*

Which is illegal to do so and has been submitting articles written against AI.

AI has not found him out.

Problem is, his research may cost him his *job, or life for that matter.*

UNSEEN FACES

The last seven season's Nathan bothered by those unseen CEO's who never show their faces? And continually sending him demands of all kinds, whether nefarious protocol, or concerning his department.
He must *daily at a set hour* receive reports on each departments progress, without fail.

There exist **six hundred and sixty-six** different operational military departments worldwide reporting to him, and other assistant's chosen by him when he's out, or on vacation.

AI'S CHOICE

The head of AI's Military is **General., David de' Mercurial,** who was seriously injured in battle against humans. *Then* when he found out about the **Robonoid** program, he volunteered which almost killed him.

It took six brain racking painful season's in years to perfect, *conflate human flesh, nano participles,* to develop a superhuman ultimate fighting Robonoid *working military machine.*
This was the template for HELL.

The trouble shooting was completed, done by AI, Nathan stepping away from this dark, evil program had enough.

Nathan's work would someday be put to the test ?

THOSE HIGHER UPS ?

All management details are done via faceless conferencing, emails never speaking to any human, or any supervisor above him ?

Nor an office manager, *not even a human or otherwise a damn rat !?*

THAT DAY IN QUESTION ?

When he was hired ten season's ago, *after submitting his application on their web site*, he downloaded his career extensive experience, forwarding to AI's hiring program.

Nathan lied about where he was born, **Texarkana, Texas** *and that he did in fact* **have parents.** **This** *would have been against him getting the job, but AI didn't know, or ignoring it, due to his experience.*

Then within seconds of submitting his resume, he was hired?

Extremely unusual but didn't matter he needed this opportunity to advance, gaining experience in his field of expertise.

Which at that youthful age loving his career, hoping to do great for mankind, would soon find this was not to be **his will, but AI's will ?**
The last emotionally difficult damn, darn frustrating years, he's come to the conclusion that his work is wrong, against humanity, against him and his fellow Texian's ?
Nathan sensing, in fact sure that in the **eye's of his spirit, that darkness**, intergrading of human **parts**, or portmanteau of cybernetic and organism as **one, is immoral**.

Leastways *within his sphere of spiritual truths*, Nathan promising himself, will find a way to destroy AI.

TAGGED WORLD

But how, AI's self awareness engulf the worldwide human network ?

Every living breathing human or animals as well insects **of all kinds are licensed, tagged with GPS IMPLANTS by AI,** and given permission to **live ?**
Their eye's have cameras, nano's can reshape into whatever they choose **too at a drop of human bloodshed !?**

Human's are worse than cockroaches to AI, infinitely hates humanity.
Nathan can't hide unless he leaves this gaged area, running too the ICE **WALL, for protection … but how ?**

NATHAN'S INVISIBLE TRACKING DEVISE

Nathan *found, discovering* a way to remove his GPS tracking implant device signature.

He replaced it with one that pretends *too, and allows him* to be visually tracked, but then the signature *evaporates, disappearing from both visual, and sound?*

Thereof, his *metahuman signature* taking on a different wave, *thus riding fluid electrical winds* waves, that's where *his signature goes.*

NATHAN'S THOUGHTS

"My device working in the same program adaptation as do, 3D visual glasses, with exception's. These evil machines Robonoids, which I'm at fault for helping AI get his way. They see the world in 3D, but not the signature of fluid energy.'
'there's unknown plethora of knowledge that I've hidden, which can be used to *beat,* defeat AI. I was told it hasn't been discovered yet ? Well, I have it my possession, as such, AI's using Tesla's Fluid energy as well, is far more advanced than my project. And is why I continue to steal from AI. Needless to say, I've invented in the last twenty season's of years, most *or all that makes all AI's working demons . "*

TESLA'S FLUID ENERGY

Nathan discovered a way to control where it goes, by sending, combing amplitude modulation, and frequency modulation, in the same carrier in that electrical fluid energy fluid scheme discovered by Tesla . *That GPS* was reformatted to fit the scheme, and untraceable nano radio waves, as they turn themselves *on,* then *off, at the speed of light.*

When they detect a tracking wave, or a 3D system's *cameras even from Nano's,* which operate on a 3D visual *process., the signature is ignited scattering into billions of trillions negative electrons in that fluid wave.*

NATHAN'S TIME, HIS GAME

On his personal time off, he rides one of his almost ancient, *2007 Electra Glide or 1946 Knucklehead Harley Davidson's*, all over Texas.

Thought it's difficult to avoid **Robonoids road checks**, this is when his personal tracking, blocking, frequency device, TBFD comes into play.

Th**ose** Robonoids camera's, or part human eye's, *designed by Nathan,* to SEE, the human's heat signature with AI's tracking system, which is based on 3D visual.

Nathan's *device makes him absolutely invisible, they don't even hear nor see his movements.*

It distorts its internal and external heat, sound, sight sensing program, blocking it's visual forward auto iris focus, at the same time since auto hearing is connected with the same configuration, **that too is blocked.**

Nano's operating under the same program and principle, falling under Nathan's distorting *sound, sight, heat signature's,* blocking construct *configuration.*

It only makes him smile when he walks around these Robonoids, and they don't see, nor hear him at all !

Nathan **hates, despises AI,** *he even put a face to this one-eyed demon. He's goal now, is to find a way to destroy, dismantling it's origins.*

Which is a dying promise, it's almost impossible to do.

The next few months off from work, Nathan heads for **Galveston, Corpus Christi, Texas**, conquering his fishing skills ..
But there's a darker catch to fishing...

The majority, not all of *world's fish is contaminated with* **Radioactivity, non-edible.,** *to the point it's dangerous to even touch, the fish caught on your line.*

This due to the *continuous on-going nuclear bombing from AI, to any, and all nation's that oppose it's intelligent design and* **perfection.**

Fish, is classified as a dangerous sport, literally.

COOL OCEAN SHORE BREEZE

Finding a nice spot camps out with Trigger, his bikes named after his horse, *a Palamino that died from eating contaminated grass.*

    On this trip Nathan hooked-on his side car, for **Tex,** his 188# English Mastiff, Great Dane, he sleeps next to Nathan, at all times.

This is his second dog as such, his first dog died a healthy *and of old age.*

Tex's a great well trained guard dog, also *attracting them ladies,* and *attacking assholes* who want him dead ?

        Only he knows why they want him dead …

    When Nathan's heads back to work, he's like **night and day, totally different man, but that Texas Cowboy hat stays on at all times.**

    A Texas Shitkicker he will forever be, *Nathan's just that.*

Another day in the life of a world who does not remember yesterday.

ANALY *TICS* IS ME

*Na*thans *the main man from Texas,* head of worldwide departments, in his study. He's that final stage, the testing of *Robonoids, simply saying, 'humans flesh integrated with machines are his final stamp of approval.*

But the end and final call belongs to AI, no hiding this from this one-eyed evil.
The last batch of *full framed humans,* men intergraded **with Robonoids machines, that were tested died.**

The Robonoid machines rejecting human flesh, despite injecting them with the proper chemicals, ignited in fire killing them, and burning the machine.
Nathan's tired of seeing this happen over and again.
They're conscience unable to handle the thought of being part human, part machine when they're awake, *or turning on the machine in them.*

They go into cardiac arrest, they die, or ignite into flames ? why.
This issue continued for many season's in years.

SEVEN OF SEVEN SEASON'S LATER

Recently Nathan emotionally exhausted heard *while on break, which could possibly be gossip or setting him,* is sitting in his regular spot watching his employee's, and listening.
One of his junior engineers talking to him.

"How y'all doing down yonder Nathan, see you ain't wearing your black cowboy hat, kinda look funny without it dude ."
"Thanks for a damn sorry ass smile dude."
"Welcome boss ."

"Next time you need to use my curbside wacker gonna tell y'all I lost it or got stolen, even though its in my barn."
"Thanks just the damn same dude. Bought one the other day on AI purchasing site, got a damn good discount by *using your name,* and where I work dude, ain't' that just damn great !"
Taking a drink of his tea, Nathan asking.

"Yeah sure, hey what's all darn damn talkin' about, *'human's* **kidnapped** *for CROP, (cybernetics robonoid organism portmanteau), what's that shit all about Mike?"*

Mike's a s**quirrely** Texan who *happens to have brains,* Nathan hired *him when no one else wanted too. They've known each other since they were kid's, attending that* **same grad school.**

Mike sharing secret's, information not known to anyone but Nathan, who already knows of this.

Nathan's mind wondering off somewhere in that Texas coast, thinking about life in a smaller retrospect.

KIDNAPPING HUMANS
Preferrable younger humans

CROP, the only worldwide engineering corporation Nathan has been working for, sends him to all their locations worldwide. Teaching others his work, something he hates doing, but he has a twisted way of teaching them.

*N*athan's the main man, the President in his department worldwide, an extremely valuable *asset to AI,* **coming very CLOSE several times, in processing, integrating human flesh with machine.**

Several times he succeeded in *fusing human flesh with machines,* then purposefully kept it to himself for reason's of morality and out of guilt.

*Fin*ally, he had to give in to AI, after sensing his fellow co- engineers knew what was going on, his *secret* **was getting closer to AI.**

In the end of it all, it paid off and he got more time off, yet he didn't care for the **accolades.**

In that breakroom another day, Mike sits next to him once more.

BREAKROOM COFFEES' SOUR

Only one robonoid has survive the integration, a female whose arms, legs were mutilated in an airplane accident, **but not really.**

The employee had lied to their superior's, this way they would get paid by undercover agents, from **CROP.**

But their plan didn't succeed and were found out, from someone up higher than the hospital's administrator. .. NATHAN.

That was when Nathan first began working on his other projects, which he did so at his home.

Nat**han** emotionally *soaked in his tears,* found he had enough, once more, witnessing all those dead human bodies.

C*ROP* didn't care how many human's they killed for their program's all kinds, using humans as **test subjects**. *Nathan asking for more time off from AI, badly needed time off, to gather, focusing on his lost morality.*

A woman from his pass, his youth was fixn' to show up, in his face. She would be that part in his life, he was missing as well from her.

They both had careers in the same building three doors down, and they never ran into each other ?

NOTE.,

This last entry hit many folks down to their boots, 'kidnaping humans' … its still happening as y'all read this. Thereof, it's one of our larger-than-life battles.

Signed., *Metal and Flesh family* . . .

AI ... *CALLS*

NATHAN JOHN

At his ranch home by the Texas Coastline, now called the GULF OF TEXAS, after that last World War, which devastated half of Mexico. Thanks to dark political forces.

Curiosity of America's Oligarch's & NGO's ?

Texas renaming the Gulf from, just because they could, and the Texas Ranger were right.+

Nathan drinking wine late evening staring at a full moon, gets a call on his <u>Alphones©</u>, *staring at it.*

*The phone's ring t*une is a horse's neighing, letting it ring a for a few seconds or more, only because it's his horse *Trigger's neigh.*
   It's stops ringing when that same caller calling him again ...
      Answering, it's AI ...
   "Nathan John, this AI calling you, we have a subject a female subject who may be perfect for your program, .. you've been hiding from me. I will let this one go. It's not called forgive and forget. I don't care about that human connection.'
   Nathan interrupting AI. ..
"Look, just tell me what you need, and what about this woman and my project I hide from you. I knew you were watching me all along, see I did this to better understand who! Who I could trust in my department, now I know. Now what about his woman ... **AI ??'**

'And how did you find my last name, it's not on any records, AI ... please do tell me."

"Nathan John, I don't have to *answer your questions at all, I answer to no one, least to say you, Nathan John.* Now about this woman. Her DNA is a match for your project and need you to get back to your project room.' 'Thereof, removing her arms, legs leaving all other body parts, then do as you do best, intergrading her body with my machines. I need this done tomorrow without fail, do I make myself clear, **human ?"**
   Nathan John not answering right quick ... when AI ordering him.

"**Nathan John,** I know you heard me human. I can see your expressions; I have eye's everywhere. I have a transporting unit being sent to you as I speak, *should be there in six minutes, don't ignore this.* You've been the most valuable asset to me the last twenty season's of years, and the only human AI, allows you to disrespect AI.'

'*to that degree you make me feel somewhat like a human. Don't like it yet needs to experience this form of disrespect.*'

'*don't forget,* Nathan John, I can take your brain transplanting in my machines anytime I choose, now I will expect you in your office in half an hour, do I make myself clear, Nathan John … ?"

Nathan John looking at **his** <u>Alphones©</u> **on top** of his wine glass ..

"I heard, understood, will be there AI."

"*One more issue,* if you continue to do your personal projects at home, I demand you download all your finding, otherwise I will kill you, do you understand me, Nathan John."

"**Hey,** I thought you already took all my projects so what's this killing stuff all about. Guess what AI, why don't you just order one of these Nano's looking at me to kill now, I'm ready to die.'

Nathan studying this one Nano, who follows him wherever he goes, landing on his left hand.

'**Well, well** ready to inject that killer juice in me, then whose gonna operate on your subject AI. No one, not one damn puppet human engineer I've trained can do, what I do best… not one AI. Even you can't with all your intelligence streaming through your hard ass hole drives … you can't do what the human spirit can, attach the Pineal Gland to a machine. For some strange reason, which I don't, nor you AI, understand you fail every time you've tired, haha ah …hmm. Could it be a 'higher power won't allow you too… could it be … AI ? *See* AI, … I've also *have* been watching your short comings, trust me on that one."

"*AI will see you in your office in twenty-five minutes.*"

"*Electronic asshole,* **I'd kick your ass if you were a dude.**"

Looking up he see's that damn platform landing, waiting for doors to up, but first it scans his face, a woman's voice *speaks to him.*

"Please enter *Doctor Nathan, we're ready to transport* you, stand still please."
                    Nathan walking in thinking to himself.

"Damn this think I can't stand it, it degenerates our bodies molecular structure, everytime it breakdown my cells. Need to remember to take heavy duty vitamins right quick when I land ."

"Dr. Nathan you should arrive to your destination, Dallas, Texas at your laboratory in seven seconds. Your staff is waiting for you, have a good trip."

Transporting to Dallas, Texas from Galveston in seven seconds, **the port** door shutting behind him . . . *when bright lights* all colors streaming horizontally, then vertically throw his body transporting Nathan is gone.

Reappearing in front of his laboratory, doors on the transporter opening, Nathan stepping out,   doors shutting behind him, *dematerializing is gone.*

Nathan looking around disappointed he's here, staring at that clock on the wall, it's 0:234 AM hour. Taking a deep, very deep sigh, when Daisy, his staff assistant **walking up to him, says.**

                    "How are you Dr. Nathan, sir ?"
            Walking off to his lab, answering her, Daisy following him.

"I was feeling great till asshole called me, then when I arrived here, *I still know I hate that asshole. And* hate **AI even more** when I'm interrupted while drinking a *damn Texas Tito's Martini any kind !* Now where's this so-called *special patient* who's so damn important to **A** fucking **I ?"**

Daisy trailing behind him warning him against him speaking with such disrespect towards AI .
"Dr. Nathan it's unwise to speak such harsh words about our employer, you'll be fired, or even disappear! *Please stop sir ."*

"**Don't** give an electrical nano ass damn!! AI knows everything about me, *you*, your dog even the color of our SHIT !! Now where's my patient Daisy take me to this woman or whatever she is ."

"*Dr. Nathan* please follow me to *AI's special room, 666*. The patient is one of our most *dedicated and intelligent* as like you, engineers."

"**Oh, really now hmm**, never heard of another one like me, ah *know this room to well, everything's gotta be that damn number !*"

Standing outside the operating ready room, doors opening automatically, they step in.
Nathan standing next to his patient when his eye's of his spirit *opening wide at her* face, his jaw drops.
Touching her face.

"*It's YOU!*"
Diasy wondering what he means by that, asking.

"*Dr. Nathan, sir.* What do you mean by that … '*it's you*' sir.*"

He continues starring at *Kathie Cythnia Lee, the woman he's loved all his life, and never forgotten her.*
Nathan now sitting on a chair looking at *her, studying her* vitals, does not answer, instead. Screams at his staff.

"*Everyone one of you leave me alone with my patient now. OUT ALL OF YOU NOW !*"
They do as they're ordered too.

Almost seventeen season's in years neither one has seen, nor heard from each other. AI, has kept them apart knowing how important they are to his projects, Nathan will soon find this out.

That AI was going to use Nathan instead of Kathie, for his project.

Following files are from momma's memory banks, I removed vital information.

Signed., Cythnia.

KATHIE CYTHNIA LEE

"**When** beauty is astoundingly forthcoming withing a *man's reach*, and that *delicate Hummingbird won't allow any man to look at her.* That **hummingbird** is protecting what it knows must not be touched. Yet, the man placing a *red liqueur sweet smelling cordial,* hoping to *capture* a warm moment with her, the *Hummingbird's sensuous finesse* knowing otherwise concealing her thoughts.'

'**In** order to fascinate *eye's of spirit along with my love, you must first be that man who can possess me with honest,* true love. *not that of hoarding my body for you selfish pleasures. Thereof, your actions are dark !'*

'**I shall** enchant with my great skills an *area* which *desires me,* allowing a righteous man to *engage in, touching my scent of love."*

KATHIE CYTHNIA LEE

Her words in her tender woman's diary, her love.

Kathie Cythnia *Lee*, a former Doctor, beautiful woman, Texas Champion Barrel Rider, *of great courage,* knowledge who *signed off,* to be used as a test. **S***he* was conscientious of the process, didn't mind being that test, *that project for Nathan. Thereof, AI demanding Nathan lie to her concerning her true condition, after the accident.*

Nathan n*ursed her back to health before moving forward, they fell in love once more, that love of their youth.*

Thereof, he wanted her to make damn SURE, about consequences, when integrating her with a machine.
        Knowing, she could have died, in the process.

Her *love for Nathan kept her alive,* as well Nathan's love for her.
        They were of one flesh, and part metal … married.

There was only one problem, **Kathie Lee** is CROP'S property, owned by unknown faces. And Nathan didn't like that at all and is that **WHY** he wants to take this company down.

Other than moral issues twisted as hell is dark.

Aside from having found out they're stealing human's for their purpose, among other things, as *in **Robonoid Army.***

It won't be easy, there are to many powerful people behind ***CROP,*** as well governments all over the world, nations have a vested interest in *this company.*

Nathan has to shut-down Kathie Lee when his working on ways to destroy this company, otherwise her system would report him to the company.

She's aware of this as well, working with him taking information, downloading it to her memory, allowing Nathan to retrieve and study.

*T*hey know that ***sooner that later***, they'll be found out, and illuminated, killed by *CROP.*

Probably even becoming a ROBONOID ??

One day when both went on their monthly vacation in Galveston, Texas "our human body is a corporeal composite entity, working in concert, with bones, blood, flesh internal components, like an orchestra finely tuned to perfection. No other machine known, designed to such intricacy not by man, but by our FATHER, CREATOR, SAVIOUR."

Signed., H.

SELLING THAT SPIRIT TO HELL

More precious than any amount of metal on this foundation, is that organ, **the Pineal Gland,** where that human conscience, that *spirit* of eye's of all humans lives.

Must be willing to give-up their Pineal Gland.

Thereof, everything falling into place when integrating flesh with machine learning, from each other, accepting who they've become.

A slave, a servant of AI, and Satan.

" ... he breathed life into man's nostrils ..."

'That which is ... 'spirit of man's eyes'
That is where the eye's of man's spirit knowing right, from evil, lives.'

That's the most important issue when combining flesh, and Robonoids as one well *oiled Satanic machine.*

"All who are willing to become their own master, and above all a part of AI's Worldwide programs ... shall know perfection in human flesh."

AI's program has a vast network of harvesting for CROP'S Programs, and stealing young adults, for their purpose, building an *Army of millions of millions of Robonoids,*

Harvesting, stealing human's for evil purposes, isn't a new program. It's been around since creation. For other evil use ...

Technology perfected itself, to the point that, the majority of humanity ignores what truly is happening, around them ?

*As well **media programs** stealing the eye's of spirit occupied, unable to focus on truths, it's Creator, Father... already knew it would be.*

Thereof, when AI, and Satan's done accomplishing their goals, another World War over humanity shall come forward.

And so it is that Nathan's Nano advancement was the foundation for all that is ???

"darkness lives, darkness is all and around all humanity, all have had of eaten of that menu."

"Darken shadows in all forms have been around before time in our eyes' of spirit ever touched the smell of life."

AI's aware of who set its foundation becoming self-aware, as such is unwilling to acknowledge a demon possessed man, ignited it's existence.

Now at a higher level of knowledge is ready to take on Satan?

Friends in places, the following short story is at our first hide-out, some twenty seasons ago.

"hope y'all are doing fine, we are to say the least, spoke to our twins today, their doing a great job creating hell, for AI.

This isn't why I'm writing Betty, so it seems our outside connection is great, Ice Wall lands are beautiful, will tell later about them.

So, know y'all know about this 'crop building, don't eat the food given y'all from AI's food processing warehouse, otherwise your eating your close's friend, not a good flavour, even with Honey Barbeque sauce… SHIT NO.

Betty gotta go, tell your family we say … howdy, can't wait till y'all arrive here, love y'all.

Cythnia msg 231226660434hram.

CROP BUILDING
that human spirit

Sun's listening to a Rooster crowing waiting for many to follow him off the cliff. On this special day pigs studying how ignorant humans can be, *happily* waiting with throats, stomach's empty.

On the menu everyday, human leftover flesh, kidney anyone?

HARVEST SEASON

The younger, heal*thier* that *human mind and flesh*, makes for a **willing,** functioning Robonoid, for AI's Army.
Eye's of that *human Spirit,* **dying** *for* **Hell,** *any takers ?*

A complete body of a young male adult, ***only,*** of eighteen season's in years, is an almost perfect candidate easier to meld, with machine's.

Male and females from birth, before harvest season and of birthing age in the harvesting tube, their *sperm* is extr*act*ed for producing more *see*ds.

T*hen*, used according to AI's production line *needs* in dep*art*ments, filling orders as needed.
  Al*so*, the harvesting of ***human internal organs*** is the highest in demand, overall other requirements.
        But there's one organ above all organs.
  The human Pineal Gland by far, the most valuable organ to AI, or Satan.

IMFP

integration of machine, and flesh program.

Kathie Lee, was chosen by Nathan, given his position with CROP-AI CORPORATION.
He fell in love with her at the moment his eyes touched the eye of her spirit.

Nathan's been given the right for CROP program master unknowns, *to make such heavy,* unemotional decisions.

They do this often to see where his devotion to CROP'S human rights stand, of which is but a lie, **there are no human rights.**

Nathan keeps his **emotions in place**, and has weathered his common sense, nailing his eye's of spirit to a deep, deep swamp from hell.

He can't take this anymore greeting all those human life's that he's authorized to *dispose of, or murdered*, and **wants out**, yet there's no out from CROP, it's *life contract.*

When you retire, they put out to die, there's no such thing.

They only way out, is to escape to the other side of the World, without being found out, or caught, then killed.

CROP, aware, allowing both to be as *one* **flesh and machine.**

They've allowed him to test the best of his knowledge under strict **CROPS MACHINE AND HUMAN INTEGRATION…. or CMHI.** **CROP-AI** owns all flesh, living, dying, born to couples as all shall be integrated with *their machines, not exceptions.*

That one heavy issue which bothers Nathan, and Kathie Lee, the integration of nano's, with her *DNA?*

Which they both designed, and regret inventing.

KITCHEN MADE FOR 2 ?

This early day is special for Nathan and Kathie Lee, their *hoping that the test she's taking comes out **positive**.*

Nathan sitting at a table with all kinds of breakfast ***fixn's,*** as he takes a sip of his coffee, *staring* with **passion** down this *long, what seems a very long* hallway, which ends with a closed door, *the bathroom.*

NANO METAL BABY?

All he can hear is **Kathie Lee,** *humming* her favorite old song from *a place in a lost history ago* ... 'A *SUMMER PLACE, by Percy Faith.*
It's one of their favorites.

After what seems like days, Nathan's motion's staring back to a time he dreadfully hates. When he first set his eyes on Katie Lee's deep blue eyes of her spirit, at the emergency room in the same building AI Technology operates out of.

Strangle enough, they get the choice of which humans that come into their emergency room, they make the decision whether they live, be used for their purpose, of not worth saving at all.

Those chosen must have special innate abilities by design, age being the most important, otherwise anyone over 30 season's **will be put down, like an animal.**
Degrees are researched as well, but do not count for much.

Intelligent individuals or given if they're educated in field fit to their standards goes up for ***review,*** then a ***decision*** will be made subject to qualifications, if needed in certain departments for **integration of machine, and flesh program.**

'NA*NO* BABIES'

Kathie Lee after almost an hour walking out of the bathroom, *Nathan's* done with his breakfast couldn't wait, is outside enjoying a glass of *Cabernet Sauvignon, also they're favorite wine.*

With all that's running through his mind when she comes up behind him, kissing his ears Nathan motionless.
Reacts to her loving gestures.

Kathie Lee *snuggling on his lap, kiss* … after awhile., *she speaks.*
Both taking a drink of their wine, …

"Well honey, love of my flesh and metal eyes, and all that other stuff built in me. Thereof, we can't tell anymore since it seems those nano's are transforming as I need by a simple thought, yet I question the infiltration of nanos' from another agency ?"

Nathan knowing what she means.

"Honey, you have stay updated, so your body's system defends itself from invaders. *You're doing that right ?"*

"Yes I know, please don't remind me. *Now* on another note please. *Since* my Robonoid body, fake flesh makes me *feel like a real horny woman,* but that thought is mine to own for now, and has to wait. **Now** I must say, 'I'm now the first pregnant flesh and *machine in history…* LOVE IT! WE'RE GONNA HAVE TWO BEAUTIFUL BABIES HONEY, ISN'T THAT WAY OUT THERE ."

"A baby, ah two babies, sounds just beautiful, we're having the first natural conceived children in this damn darn place. *Leastways* to my knowledge in the last seven or six hundred season's of years, *kissing her.* 'Guessing lets do what we love, *beside the thought of making love honey. Oh, and not way out there, in you my dear along with horrific issues headn' our way."*

Nathan, kissing her again both standing, begin walking towards their horse barn holding hands.

Saddling horse's both ride off to their favorite spot by a small creek, seating right Infront of it, and after long silence, *Kathie Lee wondering what's wrong, asking ...* .

Setting her glass of wine down grabbing his face turning it to her lips, *kissing him says.*

"**Nathan,** what's the matter, what's bothering you honey ... don't you want our babies, *please tell me what's wrong I'm worried now.*"

Both taking a deep sigh, he answers ...
               "**Familiar** with this *spot* honey?"
      "**Yes,** it's the only place where **CROP** *can't see, nor hear* us, given you've blocked their sensors, why are you asking me this. And most importantly, where we *first made love, and you proposed to me."*

      Nathan, Kathie Lee watching a quiet *streaming creek trickling away memories.*
      When **he adds,** *after a few seconds* of emotional, passionate silence from yesterdays arduous quest, between them.

"*Kathie Lee,* remember a few season's back we were *testing,* trying to combine *Nano Biometrics* with human DNA born in a test tube combining the period tables base metals with plasma liquid?"

"*Yes I do and ah hmm ...* **I see where your coming from**? *Are you saying my blood is nanoparticle's combine with plasma, and base metal as well our DNA as one ?"*
      Holding her close to him, kissing her lips.
               "Yes, dearest, yes."
      "**Honey,** *our son and daughter maybe the first born Robonoids humans on earth, born naturally of what we've been trying to create ?"*

Suddenly, both with a distant sober look, sitting across from each other, Nathan continues, seemingly changing those truths in them.

"*Honey,* yes. **I believe our project is growing in you**, hoping your not upset with me, since we both worked on this program., also I hide all the testing from AI. For our safety of course. *Besides* **we didn't know if you could even have children?** We know your having twins, my dearest last we predicted. And the last test we ran on your *blood proofs* your giving birth to two extremely healthy, powerfully strong, intelligent, boy and girl."

Kathie Lee taking one extremely large sip of her wine, refills her glass, as well **Nathan's.**

"We're in trouble, AI and **CROP** will take our twins away. *We NEED TO LEAVE AND FAST NATHAN!'*
Taking a sip, wondering ... *they hurry to find a way out of their quandary, without activating AI's security networks.*

As they continue talking about their children's future.

'*since* our children will be *metal, flesh blood, and nano's.* Will they grow in me, or will they no show, that I'm pregnant. And will it be a normal birth, or ... ? ... *how will our children come out of me?"*

Nathan drinking his wine looking at the streaming creek, answering here.

"**Good** question but first. *I knew* that the day we *got married.* I felt those *unseen faces* that render evil orders have kept an *extremely* close look at us, watching our every move. *Not only that but* I believe they already know your *pregnant* my honey dearest. And that big WHY ... *we took a month's vacation.* Yet, they've been watching our every move, *via bionano drones.* **NO! MY DEAREST NOW IS NOT THE TIME TO LEAVE.'**

 Holding each *other close kissing her lips, gazing into each others' eyes, they drop an extremely deep, ... deep sigh.*
 Nathan and Kathie Lee with **small tears running down their cheeks, he continues.**

'IF WE DO, THEY'LL HUNT US BOTH DOWN TILL THEY KILL US! *MAKING SURE THEY TAKE OUR BABIE, OR REMOVING THEM FROM YOUR BODY, DEAD OR ALIVE!! I'm NOT LETTING THIS HAPPENED AT ALL !!*

 Both exciting in a kind strange way, Nathan continues.'

'*And* another thing, we're on *WANTED POSTERS ... on the other side, and BOUNTY HUNTERS we'll get paid many, many point's to capture* our asses. We need find that right moment, then leave to the other side, **beyond the ICE WALL.** "

Holding each other close once more, Katie Lee remembering...

*"**Did we install** that fail safe shut down switch in my system, upgrading all variants, honey. I remember the download was incompatible within my female makeup. **So,** if we did... AI ALREADY KNOWS WHAT WE'RE UP TOO ... my dearest. We don't have time anymore now, we need to get my metal ass, and you fine ass up and going. .. NOW!"*

"Kathie Lee, I believe your so right, lets go!""

*Riding their horses back to their barn, Kathie Lee **wondering asking.***

"Honey wait a *moment I have something to say."*
'*Fine, ah let sit for this one, don't mind do you dear ?"*

"Ah, no. So, *I have* feeling our newborn children may have spatial nano intellect as they're nano's are binding, learning from *me, you this outside world intrigues them. their amazing nano kinesthetic inteligencija* is over the **top** !'

Ta**king** a breather sitting at the table takes a drink of orange mint tea, standing looking out their back door, sighs when she see's her horse looking at **her.**

'hmm how wonderfully beautiful horses were created to be ... hmmm ah now where was I honey ? kinda lost my next thought . . "

"Well shit, you were storming right along our kitchen so fast, I couldn't catch up with you. But you've pretty much covered all, and everything about our unborn nano babies. **So,** I'm just standing by, **'waiting** for us to get the SHIT OUTTA HERE BEFORE FREAKING AI., FINDS US. Or sends his Robonoids to kill you, then me. Then take our Nano babies with no names yet ? ah huh, hmm did you already give them a name, *Cythnia honey ?"*

Kathie Cythnia Lee, answering him.

"Listen honey Nathan pleased. ***Their constantly*** learning every darn millisecond! *Eve*n now, as I'm carrying both, they're speaking to me in languages I've never heard of, and I know all languages on this foundation ? *then* suddenly they revert to little ones in my womb, this is so strange honey.

*Our mind*s our own pattens waves of knowledge learning live in them, multiplied by a billions wave lengths of knowledge, far beyond our own.'

'*They're growth in me is speeding up*, I have feeling I may not have a normal birth, as we spoke of earlier."

"Their nano babies will continue to mature, learning, binding themselves to one another, till they become of one mind. Of course, they'll have the power to reshape into anything they chose... *anything.* I know to well, because I can do this as well*, but only with my legs, and arms."*

"Yes that I know, you've made me jump outta my boots a few times."

"John lets head out, making our way to the ICE WALL? *You've told me you found the way in, please tell yes, please!""*
Hugging Cythnia looking into her blue eyes.

"My Cythnia blue eyes, that's where we're headed love."
"Our babies will be the first humans born beyond the Ice Wall, how great is that. Thank you honey.... *Now lets go!"*

They leave they're gone towards that only opening beyond the ICE WALL. But not without complications, like AI sending Nano Robonoids attacking them in the process.

In their jet ship, Cythnia sitting right of Nathan, is sending a message to Betty.

"Guess what Betty ....
"I'm all ears sister keep on talking ...

Before Cythnia could say another word an explosion followed, Betty and family were killed by nano's.

AI IS WATCHING Y'ALL

Nathan John and Kathie Cythnia Lee and their nano babies will not be accepted, by the world or anyone.

Both brother and sister will be the closet to human perfection on this foundation leastways as close to, **Demigod's,** but in their case, also impervious to aging, and dying.

 Be them both perfecting their minds every second of their existence.

AI already knows of them and is working on killing Nathan, and Kathie, and taking their nano babies.
        Before they're born, attaching themselves to 'parents.'

This is the birth that was not even foreseen by AI, yet this is exactly what AI's been trying to do or create.

A full-fledged human and machine born of a human woman.
And capable of instantly replicating any weapon's known or unknown even too AI.

 They have the ability to destroy AI, no one knows this but AI.

FILES CONTINUES

NOT THE END

Folks depending on what comes the next few months, Cythnia or one of us will send y'all more info, mean while, stay alert, be wise out in the dark part of the foundation.

Signed., Nathan and Cythnia . . . NANO TWINS

www.ingramcontent.com/pod-product-compliance
Lightning Source LLC
LaVergne TN
LVHW051654050326
832903LV00032B/3806